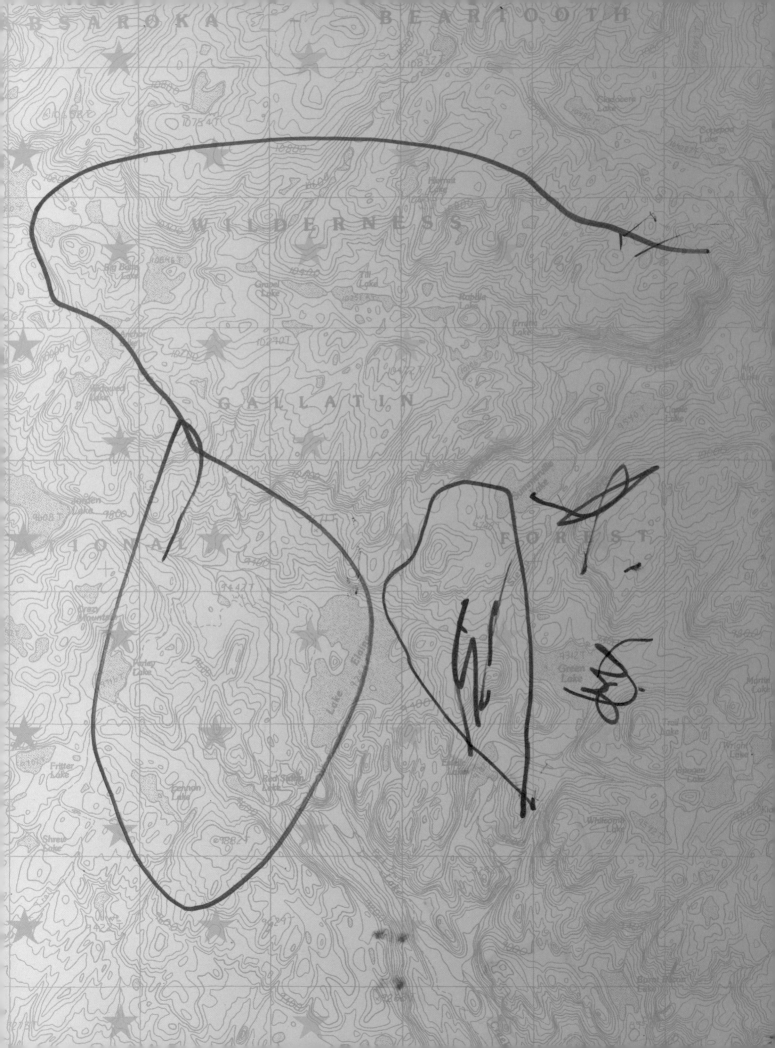

HOUGHTON MIFFLIN
SOCIAL STUDIES

★ SCHOOL AND FAMILY ★

Visit **Education Place**®
www.eduplace.com/kids

HOUGHTON MIFFLIN   BOSTON

★AUTHORS★

Senior Author
Dr. Herman J. Viola
Curator Emeritus
Smithsonian Institution

Dr. Cheryl Jennings
Project Director
Florida Institute of
    Education
University of North
    Florida

Dr. Sarah Witham
Bednarz
Associate Professor,
    Geography
Texas A&M University

Dr. Mark C. Schug
Professor and Director
Center for Economic
    Education
University of Wisconsin,
    Milwaukee

Dr. Carlos E. Cortés
Professor Emeritus, History
University of California,
Riverside

Dr. Charles S. White
Associate Professor
School of Education
Boston University

Consulting Authors
Dr. Dolores Beltran
Assistant Professor
Curriculum Instruction
California State University, Los Angeles
(Support for English Language Learners)

Dr. MaryEllen Vogt
Co-Director
California State University Center
for the Advancement of Reading
(Reading in the Content Area)

The United States has honored the Louisiana Purchase and the Lewis and Clark expedition in a new nickel series. The first nickel of the series features a rendition of the Jefferson Peace Medal. Thomas Jefferson commissioned this medal for Lewis and Clark's historic trip, which began in 1804.

Louisiana Purchase/Peace Medal nickel circulating coin images courtesy United States Mint. Used with Permission.

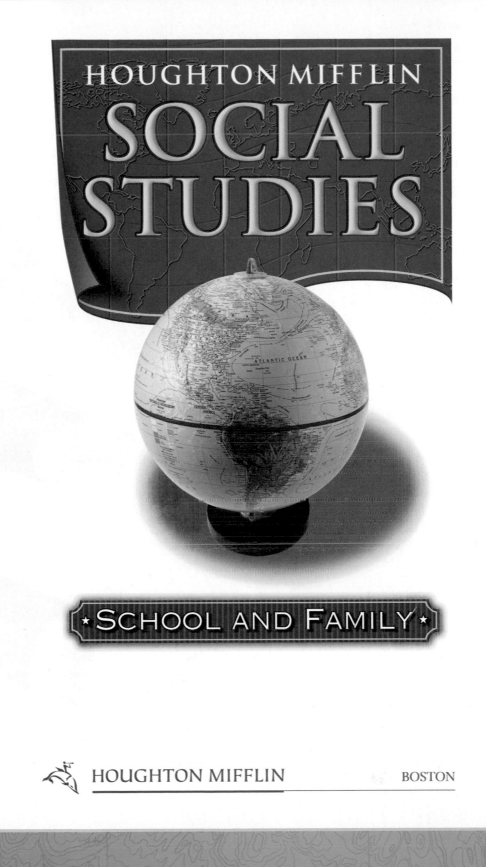

HOUGHTON MIFFLIN
SOCIAL STUDIES

★ SCHOOL AND FAMILY ★

HOUGHTON MIFFLIN   BOSTON

Consultants

Philip J. Deloria
Associate Professor
Department of History
    and Program in
    American Studies
University of Michigan

Lucien Ellington
UC Professor of Education
    and Asia Program
    Co-Director
University of Tennessee,
Chattanooga

Thelma Wills Foote
Associate Professor
University of California,
Irvine

Stephen J. Fugita
Distinguished Professor
Psychology and Ethnic
    Studies
Santa Clara University

Charles C. Haynes
Senior Scholar
First Amendment Center

Ted Hemmingway
Professor of History
The Florida Agricultural &
    Mechanical University

Douglas Monroy
Professor of History
The Colorado College

Lynette K. Oshima
Assistant Professor
Department of Language,
    Literacy and Sociocultural
    Studies and Social Studies
    Program Coordinator
University of New Mexico

Jeffrey Strickland
Assistant Professor, History
University of Texas Pan
    American

Clifford E. Trafzer
Professor of History and
    American Indian Studies
University of California,
Riverside

Teacher Reviewers

Crystal Albrecht
John Sinnott Elementary
Fremont, CA

Charlene Cook
Belair Elementary
Jefferson City, MO

Judy Jolly
Highland School
Stillman Valley, IL

Barbara Lang
Whitman Elementary
Tacoma, WA

Kay Lewis
Dalton Elementary
Aurora, CO

Anne Luckey
Oconee County Primary
    School
Watkinsville, GA

Mary Ann Preen
Seventh Avenue Elementary
Hadden Heights, NJ

Kerri Seid
Sequoia Elementary
Sacramento, CA

Elizabeth Simon
Griffin Elementary
Cooper City, FL

Printed in the U.S.A.

ISBN: 0-618-32004-0

23456789-DW-13 12 11 10 09 08 07 06 05 04

Contents

Introduction

Bringing the world to your classroom!

People Everywhere

UNIT 2 Where We Live

Vocabulary Preview
Reading Strategies: Predict and Infer, Summarize

UNIT 5 Good Citizens 226

References

Citizenship Handbook

Extend Lessons

Connect the core lesson to an important concept and dig into it. Extend your social studies knowledge!

Literature

Readers' Theater

Citizenship

Geography

Biography

More biographies at www.eduplace.com/kids/hmss05/

Economics

Primary Sources

More primary sources at www.eduplace.com/kids/hmss05/

History

Skill Lessons

Take a step-by-step approach to learning and practicing key social studies skills.

Map and Globe Skills

Chart and Graph Skills

Citizenship Skills

Reading and Thinking

Visual Learning

Maps, graphs, and charts help you learn.

About Your Textbook

❶ How It's Organized

Units The major sections of your book are units.
Each starts with a big idea.

Explore big ideas in geography, history, economics, government, and culture.

Get ready for reading.

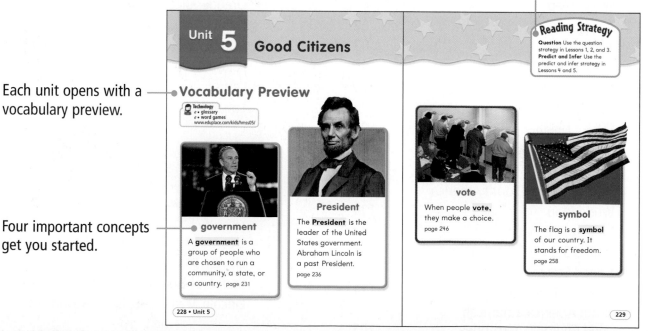

Each unit opens with a vocabulary preview.

Four important concepts get you started.

❷ Core and Extend

Lessons The lessons in your book have two parts: core and extend.

Core Lessons
Lessons bring social studies to life and help you meet your state's standards.

Core Lesson 3

Extend Lessons
Go deeper into an important topic.

Extend
Primary Sources

Core Lesson

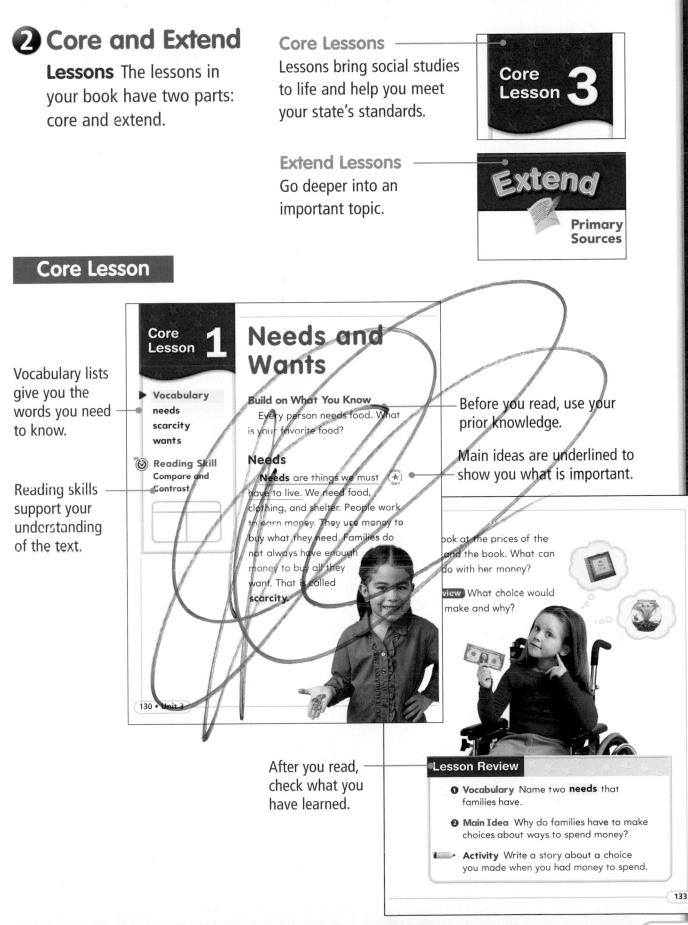

Vocabulary lists give you the words you need to know.

Reading skills support your understanding of the text.

Core Lesson 1

▶ **Vocabulary**
needs
scarcity
wants

◎ **Reading Skill**
Compare and Contrast

Needs and Wants

Build on What You Know
Every person needs food. What is your favorite food?

Needs
Needs are things we must have to live. We need food, clothing, and shelter. People work to earn money. They use money to buy what they need. Families do not always have enough money to buy all they want. That is called scarcity.

Before you read, use your prior knowledge.

Main ideas are underlined to show you what is important.

...ook at the prices of the ...and the book. What can ...do with her money?

...view What choice would ...make and why?

After you read, check what you have learned.

Lesson Review

❶ **Vocabulary** Name two needs that families have.

❷ **Main Idea** Why do families have to make choices about ways to spend money?

✏ **Activity** Write a story about a choice you made when you had money to spend.

133

130 • Unit 3

Extend Lesson   Learn more about an important topic from each core lesson.

Dig in and extend your knowledge.

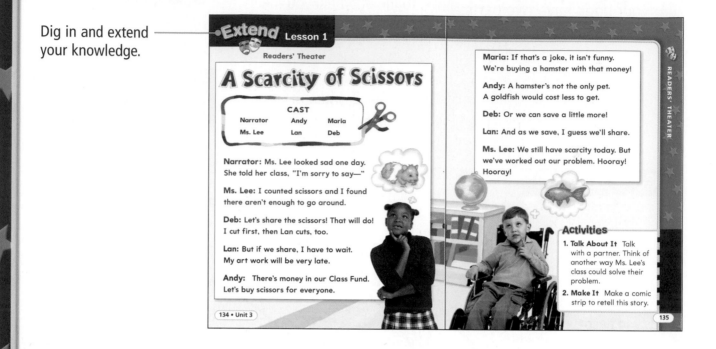

Look for literature, readers' theater, geography, economics—and more.

Write, talk, draw, and role-play!

❸ Skills

Skill Building Learn map, graph, and study skills, as well as citizenship skills for life.

Practice and apply each social studies skill.

Skill lessons step it out.

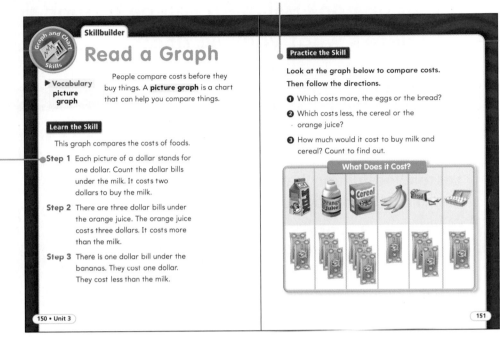

Read a Graph

Skillbuilder

▶ **Vocabulary**
picture
graph

People compare costs before they buy things. A **picture graph** is a chart that can help you compare things.

Learn the Skill

This graph compares the costs of foods.

Step 1 Each picture of a dollar stands for one dollar. Count the dollar bills under the milk. It costs two dollars to buy the milk.

Step 2 There are three dollar bills under the orange juice. The orange juice costs three dollars. It costs more than the milk.

Step 3 There is one dollar bill under the bananas. They cost one dollar. They cost less than the milk.

150 • Unit 3

Practice the Skill

Look at the graph below to compare costs. Then follow the directions.

❶ Which costs more, the eggs or the bread?

❷ Which costs less, the cereal or the orange juice?

❸ How much would it cost to buy milk and cereal? Count to find out.

What Does it Cost?

151

❹ References

Citizenship Handbook

The back of your book includes sections you'll refer to again and again.

Resources

Look for atlas maps, a glossary of social studies terms, and an index.

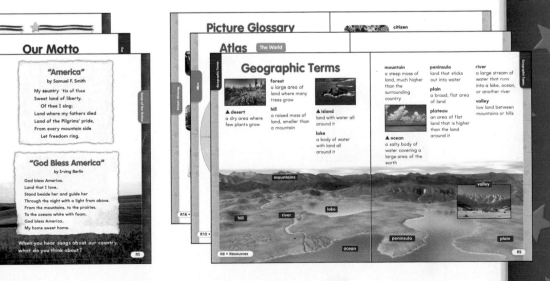

Reading Social Studies

Your book will help you be a good reader. Here's what you will find:

VOCABULARY SUPPORT

Preview Learn four important words from the unit.

Lesson Vocabulary Learn the meanings of lesson vocabulary.

Vocabulary Practice Reuse words in the reviews, skills, and extends. Show that you know your vocabulary.

READING STRATEGIES

Look for the reading strategy at the beginning of each unit.

Predict and Infer

Monitor and Clarify

Question

Summarize

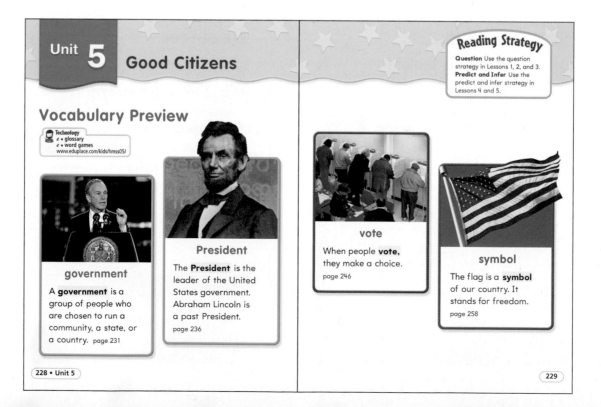

Unit **5** Good Citizens

Reading Strategy
Question Use the question strategy in Lessons 1, 2, and 3. **Predict and Infer** Use the predict and infer strategy in Lessons 4 and 5.

Vocabulary Preview

Technology
e • glossary
e • word games
www.eduplace.com/kids/hmss05/

government

A **government** is a group of people who are chosen to run a community, a state, or a country. page 231

President

The **President** is the leader of the United States government. Abraham Lincoln is a past President. page 236

vote

When people **vote,** they make a choice. page 246

symbol

The flag is a **symbol** of our country. It stands for freedom. page 258

228 • Unit 5

229

18

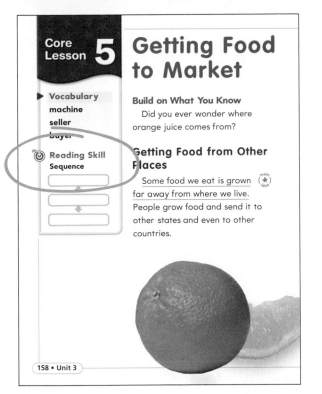

Core Lesson 5

Getting Food to Market

Vocabulary
machine
seller
buyer

Reading Skill
Sequence

Build on What You Know
Did you ever wonder where orange juice comes from?

Getting Food from Other Places
Some food we eat is grown far away from where we live. People grow food and send it to other states and even to other countries.

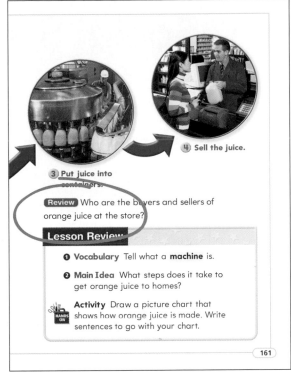

3 Put juice into containers.

4 Sell the juice.

Review Who are the buyers and sellers of orange juice at the store?

Lesson Review

❶ **Vocabulary** Tell what a **machine** is.

❷ **Main Idea** What steps does it take to get orange juice to homes?

Activity Draw a picture chart that shows how orange juice is made. Write sentences to go with your chart.

READING SKILLS

Graphic organizer
As you read, use the reading skills to organize the information.

Sequence

Cause and Effect

Compare and Contrast

Problem and Solution

Draw Conclusions

Predict Outcomes

Classify

Main Idea and Details

COMPREHENSION SUPPORT

Build On What You Know
Ask yourself what you know about the lesson topic. You may already know a lot!

Review Questions
Answer questions as you read. Did you understand what you read?

Social Studies
Why It Matters

Social Studies is exciting and fun. It is not just a book you read in school. You will use what you learn all your life.

WHEN I
- look around my neighborhood
- or read a map—
I'll use geography!

WHEN I
- save money or
- decide what to buy—
I'll use economics!

Town Map

WHEN I
- go to a neighborhood meeting
- or decide who to vote for—
I'll use what I've learned about citizenship!

WHEN I
- hear the story of a person from the past
- read books and visit museums
- look closely at the world around me—
I'll think about history!

People Everywhere

Some are very big and
Some are very small.
But it really doesn't
matter at all.
Because a family is
a family.

—From "A Family is a Family"
by Skip West

The Big Idea

What do we learn
from our families,
our schools, and
our communities?

Vocabulary Preview

Technology
e • glossary
e • word games
www.eduplace.com/kids/hmss05/

leader

Your teacher is the **leader** of your class.

page 44

family

People in a **family** care about each other.

page 26

Reading Strategy

Predict and Infer Use the predict and infer strategy in Lessons 1, 2, and 3.
Summarize Use the summarize strategy in Lessons 4 and 5.

community

Your home and school are part of the **community** where you live. page 54

country

The United States is the **country** where you live. page 60

Family

Build on What You Know

You are part of a family. Who are the people in your family?

A Family of Helpers

A **family** is a group of people who care about each other. People in a family help each other. Everyone in a family can be a helper.

main idea

Everyone is a family helper.

Families work together.

Family work can be fun.

Review What does your family do together?

Families Learn Together

You learn many things from your family. Your family can teach you how to care about other people. Your family can teach you how to be safe and healthy.

(★) main idea

Families care.

Families help us to learn to do things.

Families share stories.

Review What do you learn from your family?

Lesson Review

① **Vocabulary** What is a **family**?

② **Main Idea** Tell about how people in a family can help each other.

HANDS ON **Activity** Draw a picture of your family.

Literature (Read Aloud)

JINGLE DANCER

by Cynthia Leitich Smith

Activities

1. **Talk About It** Tell about something you learned from your family.

2. **Write About It** Write a sentence about Jenna in this story.

Read a Calendar

▶ **Vocabulary**
calendar

You can find special days on a calendar. A **calendar** shows the months of the year, the weeks in a month, and the days of the week.

Learn the Skill

Step 1 There are twelve months in a year. Name the months.

Step 2 Read the days of the week on the calendar.

Step 3 Each day in a month has a number. How many days are in November?

Use the calendar to answer the questions.

1 What special day is November 7th?

2 Which holiday is on a Thursday in November?

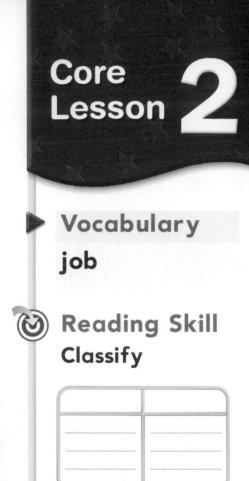

Core Lesson 2

In Your Classroom

Vocabulary
job

Reading Skill
Classify

Build on What You Know

Look around you. There are many children in your classroom. Think about caring for others.

Caring About Others

We learn to work together in a class. We treat each other nicely. We help each other. Helping others shows we care.

main idea

Children help on the playground.

Helping in the Classroom

There are jobs to do at school. A **job** is work to be done. Your classroom has helpers to get jobs done.

main
(★)
idea

Review Why do we have classroom helpers?

Saying the Pledge of Allegiance

At school we show that we care about each other. <u>When we say the "Pledge of Allegiance," we show that we care about our country.</u>

main idea

Skill **Reading Visuals** Why are the children and the teacher holding their hands on their chests?

The Pledge of Allegiance

I pledge allegiance to the flag
of the United States of America
and to the Republic for which it stands,
one Nation under God, indivisible,
With liberty and justice for all.

Review Why do we say the "Pledge of Allegiance"?

Lesson Review

❶ **Vocabulary** Write or tell about a **job** you do at school.

❷ **Main Idea** What are ways you show that you care about others in your class?

Activity Draw a picture of your class saying the Pledge of Allegiance.

HANDS ON

Citizenship

Helping Hands

Think about ways you can be a helper.

We Help Song

We help with jobs at home,
We put our things away,
We use our helping hands,
We use them every day.

We help with jobs at school,
We help each other out,
We use our helping hands,
And that's what it's all about!

Make a Helping Hands Tree

You will need:

Step 1. Trace your hand on a piece of paper. Then cut out the paper hand.

Step 2. Write one helping job you can do on the paper hand.

Step 3. Hang your helping hand on the tree.

Compare Pictures and Maps

▶ **Vocabulary**

map

A **map** is a drawing of a place. The pictures on a map show where things are.

Learn the Skill

Step 1 This photo shows what a zoo looks like if you are looking down at it from above.

Step 2 Look at the map of the zoo on the next page. The map shows the buildings and paths you see in the photo.

Step 3 Look at the photo. Then look at the map. The things on the map and in the photo are in the same places.

San Diego Zoo

Practice the Skill

Compare the photo and the map of the zoo.

1 Tell how the map and the photo are the same.

2 Tell how the map and the photo are different.

San Diego Zoo

► **Vocabulary**
leader
rule

Reading Skill
Compare and
Contrast

Leaders and Rules

Build on What You Know

Have you played the game Follow the Leader? What do you think a leader does?

Leaders

Every group needs a leader. Parents are leaders in a family. Your teacher is a leader. A **leader** helps a group work well together.

main idea (★)

Leaders Make Rules

Leaders make rules that help people.

A **rule** tells people what they should do.

Rules help keep things fair for everyone.

Rules help keep people safe.

main idea ★

PLAYGROUND RULES

☑ Sit on slide
☑ Sit on swings
☑ No dogs here

Review Why do leaders make rules?

Following Rules

You have rules at home and in school. When everyone follows the rules, things are fair for everyone. It is important to follow the rules.

Review Why is it important for everyone to follow the rules?

Lesson Review

1 Vocabulary Tell about one school **rule.**

2 Main Idea Why do groups need leaders?

HANDS ON **Activity** Make a sign that shows a rule at home.

Literature (Read Aloud)

The Saturday Escape
by Daniel J. Mahoney

In this story three friends
sneak out to the library
story hour without
doing their
Saturday chores.

Jack wondered what his mother would say
when she saw his room. His parents were
always so proud of him when he cleaned up.
His mother kissed him and said, "Good boy,"
and his father scratched him behind the ears.
Jack did not think that would happen today.

Melden, too, was wondering about what was happening at home. His parents had trusted him to paint the shutters. He could imagine only too well what the house would look like when his brothers were done.

Angie was remembering her piano recital. Her dad had been so proud of her that night, and he'd gone to a lot of trouble to tape her performance. But how proud of her would he be today, when he found out she wasn't really practicing?

As the story ended, Jack stood up. "May I be excused?" he asked.

"But story hour isn't over yet," the storyteller told him.

"I know," said Jack, "but I just thought of something I have to do."

"And I have to help him," said Angie.

"Me, too," said Melden.

"We'll be right back," Jack promised, and the three friends hurried out of the library.

First they went to Melden's house. Luckily, his brothers had painted each other instead of the shutters.

Then they went to Angie's house, so she could finish practicing. Jack and Melden enjoyed the music. So did Angie's dad.

Finally, they went to Jack's house and cleaned his room. They felt very proud of themselves. But now that all the painting and practicing and picking up was done, it was too late to go back to story hour.

So they had one of their own!

Activities

1. **Talk About It** Why do you think Jack, Angie, and Melden went home to finish their chores?

2. **Write About It** Write a sentence about what you liked best in the story.

![Map and Globe Skills]

Read a Map Key

▶ **Vocabulary**
map key
symbols

A map can show where places are in a neighborhood. A **map key** helps you find the places.

Learn the Skill

Step 1 The places and things on a map key are shown by symbols. **Symbols** are pictures that stand for real things.

Step 2 Look at each symbol on the map key. Read the words. What real thing does each symbol stand for?

Step 3 Find a house symbol on the map. Each house symbol shows where a real house is.

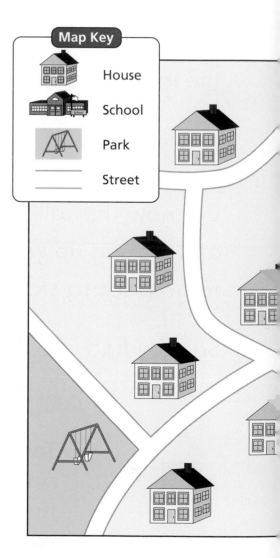

Map Key

House

School

Park

Street

Look at the map and the map key.

1 Choose a symbol on the map. Use the map key to tell what the symbol stands for.

2 Use your finger to trace a route between the school and the park.

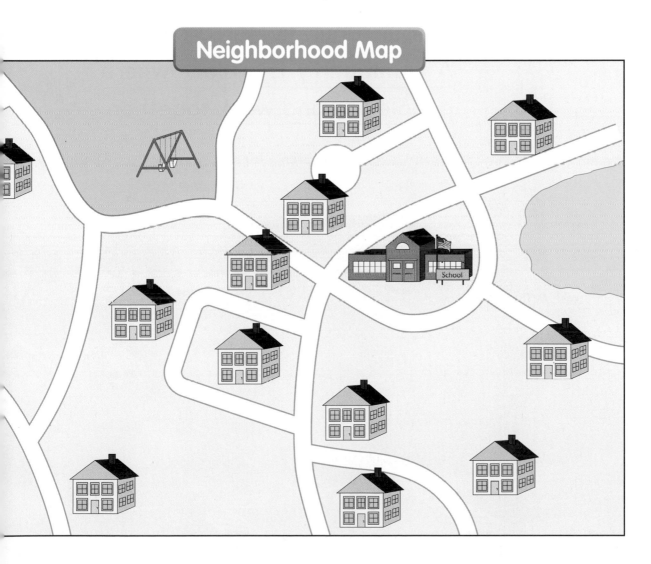

Neighborhood Map

A Community

Build on What You Know

Are there fire stations and schools near where you live? Who are the people who work nearby?

Vocabulary
community

Reading Skill
Classify

Community Life

Your family lives in a community. A **community** is a place where people live and work together.

main idea

Community Helpers

You help at home and at school. Communities have helpers too. <u>Helpers do jobs that make the community a nice place to be.</u> Some helpers keep us safe. Others help keep a community clean.

(★) main idea

Rosemary Cloud is a fire chief in Georgia.

Catherine Beyers is a librarian in Wisconsin.

Review Why are helpers important in the community?

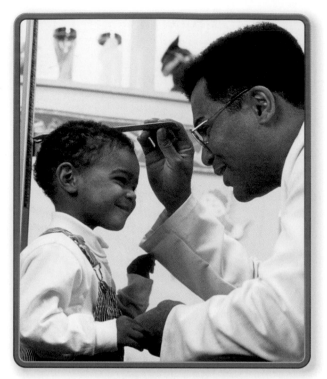

Nurses and doctors help us stay healthy.

Workers help keep a community looking nice.

Postal workers make sure people get their mail.

Community Places

A community has many places where people can go. Your school is a place in your community. A community can have a library and a hospital. Some communities have a center where all people can go.

Review What places in your community have you been to?

Lesson Review

❶ **Vocabulary** Name three places in your **community.**

❷ **Main Idea** What do community helpers do?

Activity Choose a community helper. Act out what that helper does. Ask a classmate to guess who you are.

FIRE CHIEF ROSEMARY CLOUD

Chief Cloud says, "Helping people is the thing I like best."

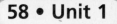

Let's meet a community helper with a big job. Rosemary Cloud is the fire chief in East Point, Georgia. Rosemary Cloud is the first African American woman in the United States to become a fire chief.

Activities

1. **Talk About It** Tell how firefighters show they care.

2. **Read About It** Look in your library for a book about firefighters.

Visit Education Place for more biographies. www.eduplace.com/ kids/hmss05/

Moving to New Homes

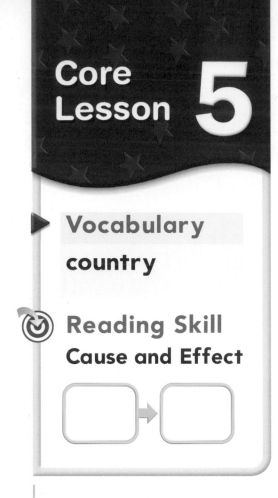

Build on What You Know

Has your family ever moved to a new place? How did your life change in the new place?

Families Move

Many families move from one place to another. Sometimes a family moves to the United States from another country. A **country** is a land with its own people, leaders, and its own rules.

main idea

Why People Move

People move for different reasons. Some  people move to get better jobs. Some people move to be near their family.

Meet the Lemos family. Katia and Timoteo Lemos moved to the United States from Brazil. They moved to find better jobs.

The Lemos family lives in Massachusetts.

Skill **Reading Maps** Trace the route from Brazil to the United States. What ocean do you cross?

Review Why do you think it would be hard at first to move to a new country?

Moving to the United States

Long ago, many people came to North America from different countries. People are still coming to the United States with new ideas and new ways of living.

People Moving to the United States	
In 1960, most people came from these countries:	In 2000, most people came from these countries:
Italy Germany Canada Great Britain Poland	Mexico Philippines China India Cuba

New People Bring New Things

A community can learn new things when people move there. People bring their language. They bring their music and clothing. They bring their special foods.

Review What do people bring with them when they move to another country?

Lesson Review

❶ Vocabulary Tell about someone you know who moved here from another **country.**

❷ Main Idea Why do people move?

HANDS ON **Activity** Make a poster showing ways you could welcome a new classmate.

Moving Then and Now

Many years ago people moved in wagons pulled by strong animals. The wagons were small. Families could bring only a few things.

Today many families can use big trucks to move to a new place. Now people can take most of their things.

Activities

1. **Draw It** Draw pictures of things you would take to a new home.

2. **Write About It** Write a sentence about moving then and now.

Big Idea

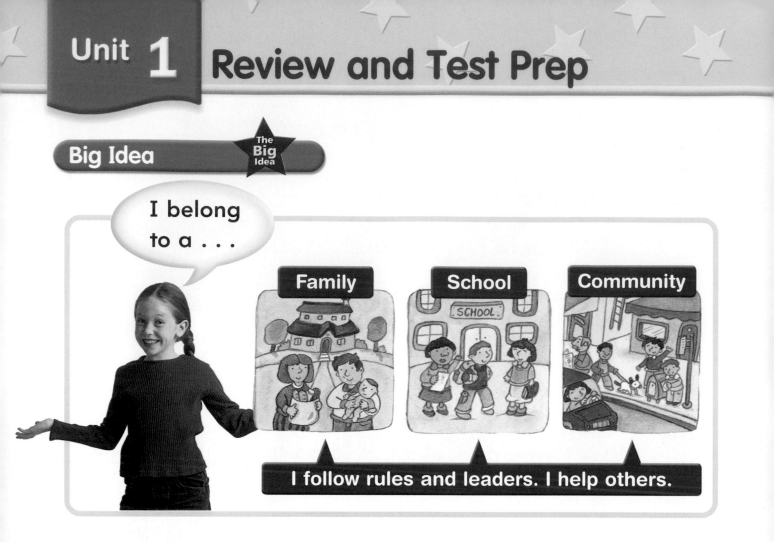

I belong to a . . .

Family   School   Community

I follow rules and leaders. I help others.

Tell the words that are missing from the sentence.

1. You belong to a _____ , a _____ , and a _____ .
(pages 26, 36 and 54)

2. At school you follow _____ and _____ .
(pages 44 and 45)

Facts and Main Ideas

3. Who are the leaders at your home and school?
(pages 44 and 45)

4. What are some home and school rules? (page 46)

5. Who are some community helpers? (pages 55 and 56)

Write the letter or word for each correct answer.

6. A person who helps others work together

7. Something that tells people what they must do

8. A group of people who care about each other

9. Work that a person can do

A. **country** (page 60)

B. **rule** (page 45)

C. **job** (page 37)

D. **leader** (page 44)

E. **family** (page 26)

✔ Test Practice

10. What does the word **community** mean?

   A. a classroom job

   B. a rule for many people to follow

   C. a place where people live and work

   D. a school leader

Critical Thinking

Compare and Contrast

11. Which rules at home are different from school rules?
   (page 46)

Skillbuilders

Read a Calendar

12. What month does this calendar show?

13. What day is Memorial Day?

14. How many days are there between May 10 and May 17?

Read a Map Key

15. How many benches are in Oak Park?

16. What is the symbol for garden in the map key?

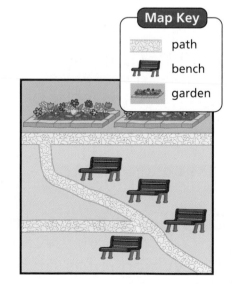

Community Helper Puppets

Think of some helpers in your community.

❶ Draw a picture of a community helper.

❷ Cut and paste the helper to a stick.

❸ Have your puppet talk about its work.

In Your Classroom

Look for these Social Studies Independent Books in your classroom.

CURRENT EVENTS
WEEKLY (WR) READER

Current Events Project

Create a **People in the News** report. Find current events from Weekly Reader on the social studies website.

The President gave a speech Today. He talked about jobs.

Technology
Current Events Project
www.eduplace.com/kids/hmss05/

At the Library

Look for these books at your library.

On the Town: A Community Adventure
by Judith Caseley

Jalapeño Bagels
by Natasha Wing

Where We Live

Don't you think that someone had a very funny notion to go and name our planet *Earth* when most of it is ocean?

"Our Planet Earth"
by Aileen Fisher

The Big Idea

What do you know about Earth and its people?

Unit 2 Where We Live

Vocabulary Preview

Technology
e • **glossary**
e • **word games**
www.eduplace.com/kids/hmss05/

continent

A **continent** is a very large area of land. The continent where you live is called North America.

page 76

mountain

A **mountain** is land that is higher than all other land around it. page 82

Reading Strategy

Predict and Infer Use the predict and infer strategy in Lessons 1, 2, 3, and 4.
Summarize Use the summarize strategy in Lessons 5, 6, and 7.

natural resource

Water is a **natural resource** that people use every day. page 88

season

Summer is a **season** that can have hot weather. page 97

Core Lesson 1

Our Earth

Vocabulary

ocean

continent

Reading Skill
Compare and
Contrast

Build on What You Know

The world is where you live. What do you know about the world?

Earth, Our World

Earth is another name for the world where we live. It is made up of land and water. The globe shows Earth's land and water.

main idea ★

A globe is a model of Earth.

Ocean

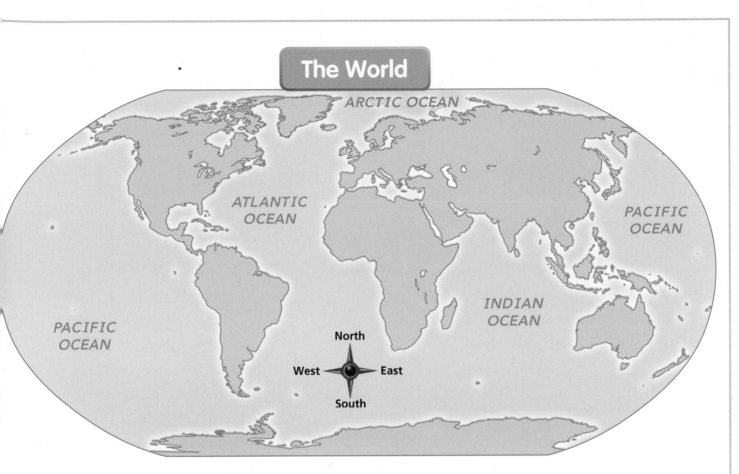

The World

ARCTIC OCEAN

ATLANTIC
OCEAN

PACIFIC
OCEAN

PACIFIC
OCEAN

INDIAN
OCEAN

North

West — East

South

Skill **Reading Maps** How can you tell land from ocean on this map?

Oceans

There is more water than land on Earth. The areas of water on the globe and on the map are oceans. An **ocean** is a large body of salty water. Earth has four oceans.

main idea (★)

Review In what way is a globe like Earth?

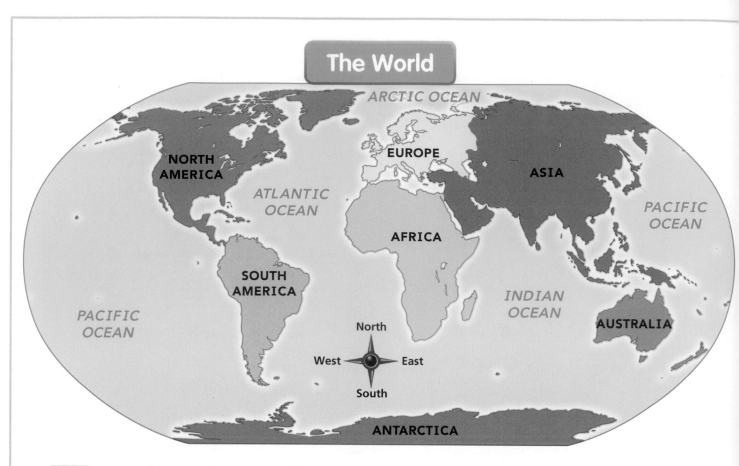

The World

ARCTIC OCEAN

NORTH
AMERICA

EUROPE

ASIA

ATLANTIC
OCEAN

PACIFIC
OCEAN

AFRICA

SOUTH
AMERICA

North

PACIFIC
OCEAN

West ← ★ → East

INDIAN
OCEAN

AUSTRALIA

South

ANTARCTICA

Skill **Reading Maps** What are the names of the continents?

Continents

A very large area of land is called a **continent.** Earth has seven continents. Find them on the map. Our country is part of the continent called North America.

main ⭐ *idea*

Review Which oceans touch North America?

Continents	Oceans
North America	Pacific Ocean
South America	Atlantic Ocean
Africa	Arctic Ocean
Europe	Indian Ocean
Australia	
Antarctica	
Asia	

Lesson Review

❶ **Vocabulary** Tell something you know about **continents** and **oceans.**

❷ **Main Idea** What do we call the areas of land and water that we see on a globe?

✏ **Activity** Write a sentence telling what continent you live on.

The Pacific Ocean

PACIFIC OCEAN

Let's explore the world's biggest ocean. It touches the five continents of North America, South America, Antarctica, Australia, and Asia.

There is a big colorful world of plants and animals under the ocean waves.

The ocean floor can be hilly or flat. Big volcanoes rise from deep in the Earth.

Activities

1. **Talk About It** Talk about what you see in the ocean.

2. **Create It** Cut and paste colored paper to make a picture of the ocean floor, plants, and animals.

Skillbuilder

Compare Globes and Maps

▶ **Vocabulary**
globe

We all live on Earth. Earth is round like a ball.

Learn the Skill

A **globe** is a model of Earth. A model is something small that looks just like a bigger object.

Step 1 The globe is round like a ball. The blue parts of the globe show water. The other color areas show the land.

Step 2 Look at the map of the world. It is flat. It shows Earth's land and water too. Find some water and some land on the world map.

Look at the globe and the map of the world.

1 Tell two ways that the globe and the map of the world are the same.

2 Tell one way that they are different.

The World

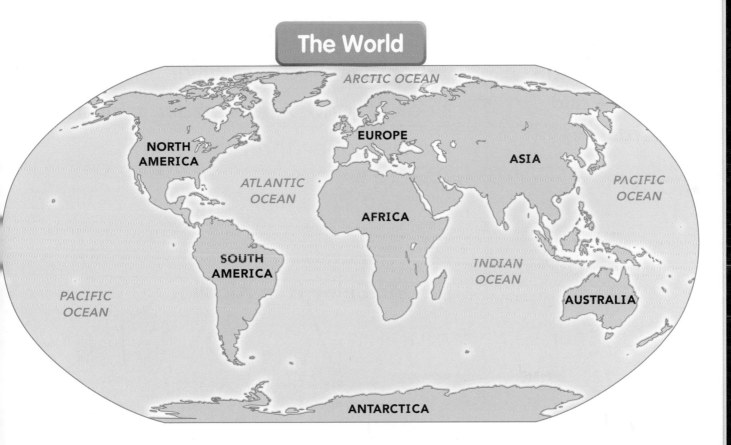

Our Land, Our Water

▶ **Vocabulary**
mountain
plain
river
lake

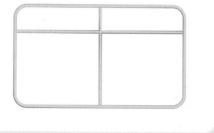

Reading Skill
Compare and Contrast

Build on What You Know
Think of the land around your school. Is it flat or hilly?

Mountains and Plains

Earth is made up of different kinds of land. A **mountain** is land that is higher than the land around it.

main idea ⭐

Mt. McKinley is in Alaska.

ALASKA

A **plain** is a large, flat land area. Some plains are grassy. Other plains have good soil for farming. Plains can be high land or low land.

(Review) What do you know about mountains and plains?

Nebraska has high grassy plains.

NEBRASKA

Rivers and Lakes

Earth has different kinds of water. A **river** is fresh water that moves across the land to the ocean. The Mississippi River is one of the longest rivers in the United States.

Steamboats carry people and things on the Mississippi River.

A **lake** is a body of water that has land around it. Some lakes are huge. Look at the map of the Great Lakes.

GREAT LAKES

Review What is the difference between a river and a lake?

Lesson Review

❶ **Vocabulary** Tell how a **river** is different from a **lake.**

❷ **Main Idea** What kind of land and water can you find on Earth?

HANDS ON **Activity** Draw a picture showing plains and mountains.

John Muir

John Muir liked to walk in the woods and fields. He loved to learn about plants and animals.

Yosemite Valley was one of John's favorite places. He wrote articles telling people that it should be a national park. In 1890 John's dream came true. One day you might visit Yosemite National Park in California.

Activities

1. Talk About It Tell in your own words why people remember John Muir.

2. Write About It Write about something you have seen in nature.

Visit Education Place for more biographies. www.eduplace.com/kids/hmss05/

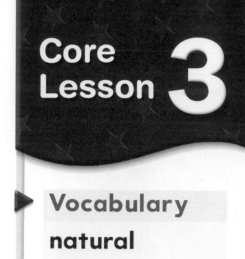

Natural Resources

Build on What You Know

People use water and wood every day in many different ways. You use wooden pencils and you drink water.

Earth Has Natural Resources

Plants, soil, and water come from nature. Earth has natural resources. A **natural resource** *main idea* is something in nature that people use.

Review What things do you see in your classroom that come from wood?

People Use and Save Resources

Oil and coal are found (★ main idea) under the ground. People can use those natural resources to heat homes and buildings. Oil can be made into gasoline. People use gasoline in their cars.

This man is digging coal under the ground.

These children pick up trash that could wash back into the ocean.

Many people work to save natural resources such as water. They also work to replace trees that have been cut down.

Review What can you do to save water and other natural resources?

Lesson Review

1 **Vocabulary** Tell something you know about a **natural resource.**

2 **Main Idea** What do people do with natural resources?

 Activity Use pictures and words to make a poster that shows people working to save water.

What Comes from Trees?

Trees are an important natural resource. Many things you see and use every day come from trees.

Wood can be used to make pencils.

Fruits such as apples and peaches come from trees.

The frame and shingles of this house are made from wood.

Wood can be ground into pulp to make paper for books.

Violins are made from wood.

Wood can be shaped into furniture.

Activities

1. **Write About It** Make a list of things you see in your classroom that come from trees.

2. **Make It** Draw pictures or use magazines to make a mobile that shows the many things that come from trees.

Read a Chart

▶ **Vocabulary**
chart

Charts use words or pictures to show information.

Read the **chart** to find out how people use natural resources.

Learn the Skill

Step 1 The title tells you that this chart is about natural resources.

Step 2 The labels under the title tell what information is in the chart. The labels show ways people use plant and water resources.

Step 3 Look at the first row of pictures on the chart. You see trees used for wood. What is the water used for?

Practice the Skill

Read the chart. Answer the questions.

1 What are some ways people use plants as natural resources?

2 What are some ways people use water resources?

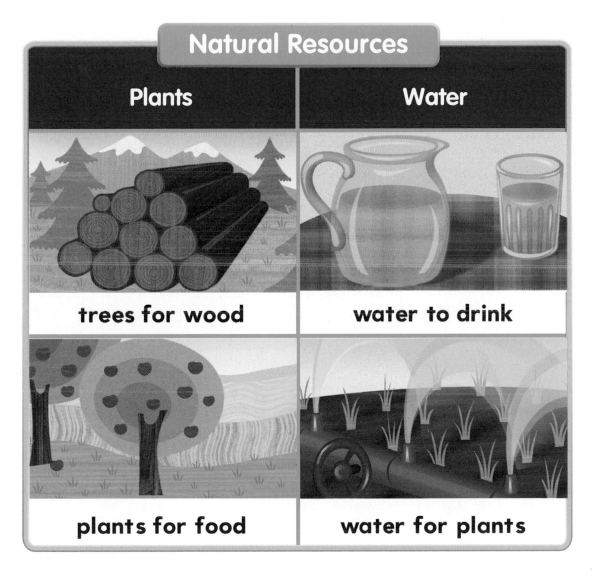

Natural Resources

Plants	Water
trees for wood	water to drink
plants for food	water for plants

Weather and Seasons

Build on What You Know

Look out the window. Is it sunny or cloudy? People like sunny days for working and playing outside.

Weather

Weather is what it is like outside. Weather is always moving and changing. Winds cause the weather to change. Rain, wind, clouds, and temperature are all part of weather.

main idea ⭐

sunny   rainy   snowy   cloudy

Seasons

A **season** is a time of the year. Fall, winter, spring, and summer are the four seasons. Each season has different weather.

Review What season is it now?

Dressing for the Weather

Seasons and weather change how people live. Children wear warm clothes in cold weather. They can go to the beach in hot weather. People may have to change their clothes because of weather.

In the United States, winter can be cold or hot. It depends on where you live.

Los Angeles

Temperatures on a February Day	
Miami, Florida	73°
Chicago, Illinois	30°
Los Angeles, California	65°
Atlanta, Georgia	57°

Review What is winter weather like where you live?

Chicago

Atlanta

Miami

Lesson Review

❶ **Vocabulary** Write a sentence using the words **weather** and **season.**

❷ **Main Idea** In what ways does weather change how people live each season?

Activity Make a picture book about the four seasons where you live.

What Will the Weather Be?

Then

Long ago, there were no weather reports. People could not find out if rain or snow were coming. They did have some old weather sayings.

Cows lying down
Good chance of rain

If anthills are high in July,
Winter will be stormy.

Now

Today weather reporters find out what the weather will be. They use satellites and computers. Satellites take pictures of weather across the world. The pictures show where big storms are.

Activities

1. **Create It** Make a chart that shows all the days of the week. Write or draw pictures that show what the weather is like each day.

2. **Read About It** Find books about weather at the library.

City, Town, Suburb

▶ **Vocabulary**
city
town
suburb

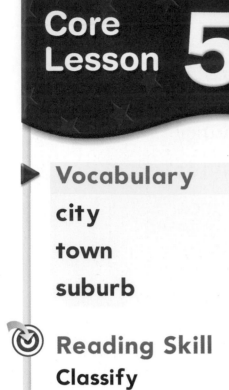

Reading Skill
Classify

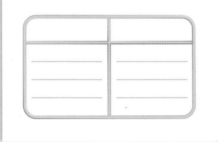

Build on What You Know

What does your community look like?

Living in a City

A **city** has many people and buildings that are very close together. A city is a busy community. A city has many streets, and places to shop and eat. Many people live and work in cities.

main idea

San Francisco, California

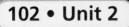

The main street of a town

Living in a Town

A **town** is a smaller community than a city. Houses and buildings are not as close together. There are fewer people, shops, and streets.

A **suburb** is a town that is close to a city. Some towns and suburbs have farms.

(Review) How are cities different from towns?

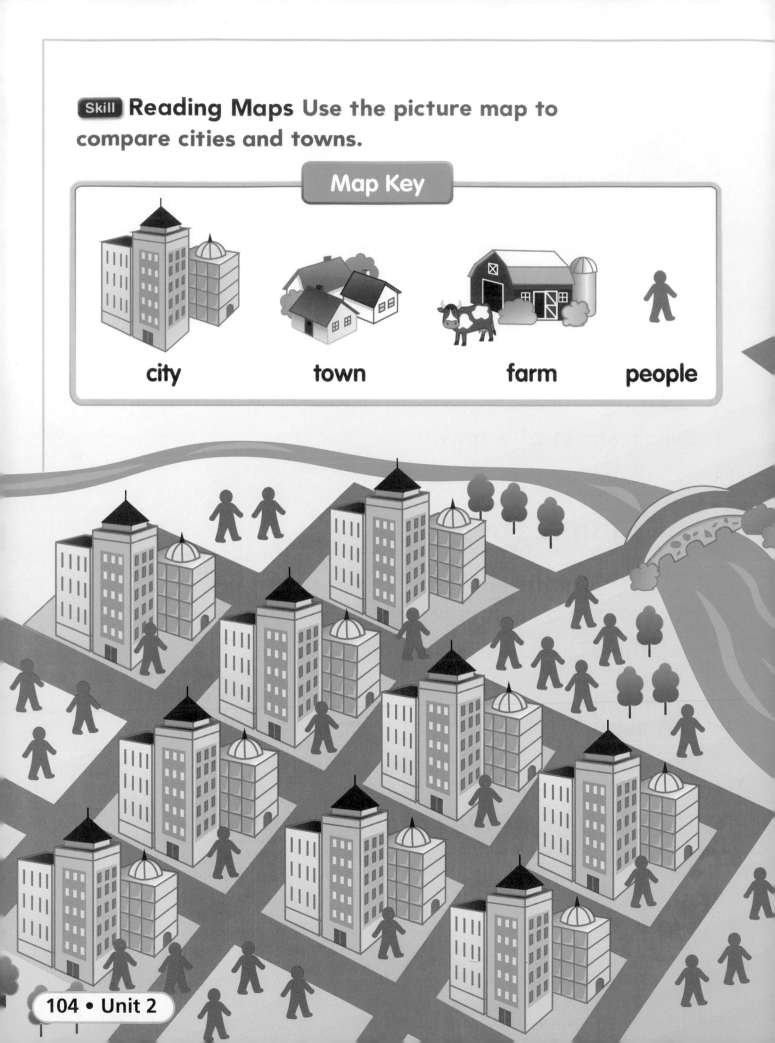

Skill **Reading Maps** Use the picture map to compare cities and towns.

Map Key

city   town   farm   people

Lesson Review

❶ Vocabulary Tell something you know about a **city.**

❷ Main Idea Use the map to tell the differences between a city and a town.

Activity Write about your community. Tell if it is a city, suburb, or town. Tell about some places in your community.

Small Town, Big City

Can you believe that this big city used to be a small town?

Here is San Francisco today. It is built on hills by the water. Millions of people live here. There are skyscrapers, bridges, homes, trains, boats, and cars. What else is different than long ago?

This is a picture of San Francisco about 150 years ago. It was a small town by the water. Fewer than 1000 people lived here. There were only a few small houses. You can count the number of roads you see.

Activities

1. **Talk About It** Tell ways a town grows to become a city.

2. **Build It** Build a model of a town long ago and a city today.

107

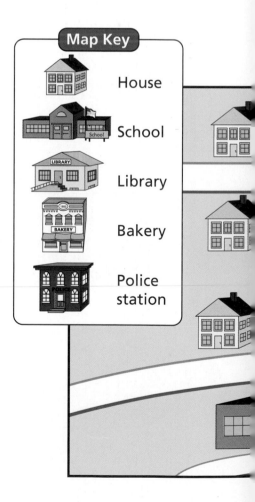

Skillbuilder

Find Near and Far

▶ **Vocabulary**
distance

Maps show the distance between things. **Distance** is the measure of how near or far something is from one place, or point.

Learn the Skill

Step 1 The school is one place, or point, on the map. Put your finger on the school.

Step 2 Put another finger on the police station. The police station is near the school.

Step 3 Now look at the library. The library is far from the school.

Map Key

House

School

Library

Bakery

Police station

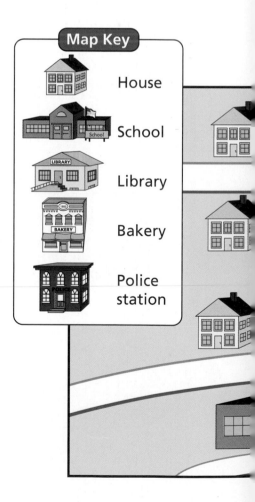

Follow the directions to compare distance.

❶ Put one finger on the school. Put another finger on the bakery. Is the bakery near or far from the school?

❷ Look at the bakery. Is the library near or far from the bakery?

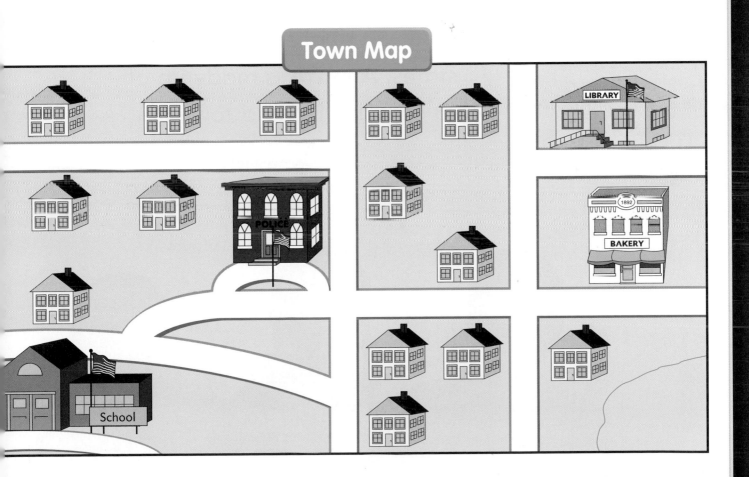

Town Map

Our Country

Vocabulary

state

citizen

Reading Skill
Main Idea and Details

Build on What You Know

Do you know the name of our country?

The United States

Our country is called the United States of America. Look at the map. The United States is made up of 50 smaller parts called states. A **state** is made up of cities, suburbs, and towns.

main idea

United States

ALASKA

WASHINGTON
OREGON
IDAHO
MONTANA
NORTH DAKOTA
MINNESOTA
SOUTH DAKOTA
WISCONSIN
MICHIGAN
NEW HAMPSHIRE
VERMONT
MAINE
MASSACHUSETTS
NEW YORK
RHODE ISLAND
CONNECTICUT
NEW JERSEY
DELAWARE
MARYLAND
WYOMING
NEVADA
UTAH
COLORADO
NEBRASKA
IOWA
ILLINOIS
INDIANA
OHIO
WEST VIRGINIA
PENNSYLVANIA
VIRGINIA
CALIFORNIA
ARIZONA
NEW MEXICO
KANSAS
MISSOURI
KENTUCKY
TENNESSEE
NORTH CAROLINA
OKLAHOMA
ARKANSAS
SOUTH CAROLINA
ALABAMA
GEORGIA
MISSISSIPPI
TEXAS
LOUISIANA
FLORIDA
PACIFIC OCEAN
ATLANTIC OCEAN
Gulf of Mexico
HAWAII

Skill **Reading Maps** Where is your state?

You Are a Citizen

You are a citizen of the state where you live and the country where you were born. A **citizen** is someone who belongs to a community, a state, or a country.

main idea

Review Which state are you a citizen of?

Land and Water in the United States

Each state has different kinds of land and water. The United States is a big country. It stretches from the Atlantic Ocean to the Pacific Ocean.

main idea ★

California: The Sierra Nevada is a group of mountains in the state of California.

Florida has ocean beaches and lakes.

Illinois: The states in the middle of the country have farmland, lakes, and rivers.

New York: The biggest city in New York state is New York city. It has a busy harbor.

Review How can you tell that the United States is a big country?

Lesson Review

1 Vocabulary Use the words **citizen** and **state** in a sentence.

2 Main Idea How many states are in the United States?

Activity Write a sentence about your state. Tell why you like living there.

Make a Passport

People from the United States must have a passport to visit other countries. A passport shows the country where you live.

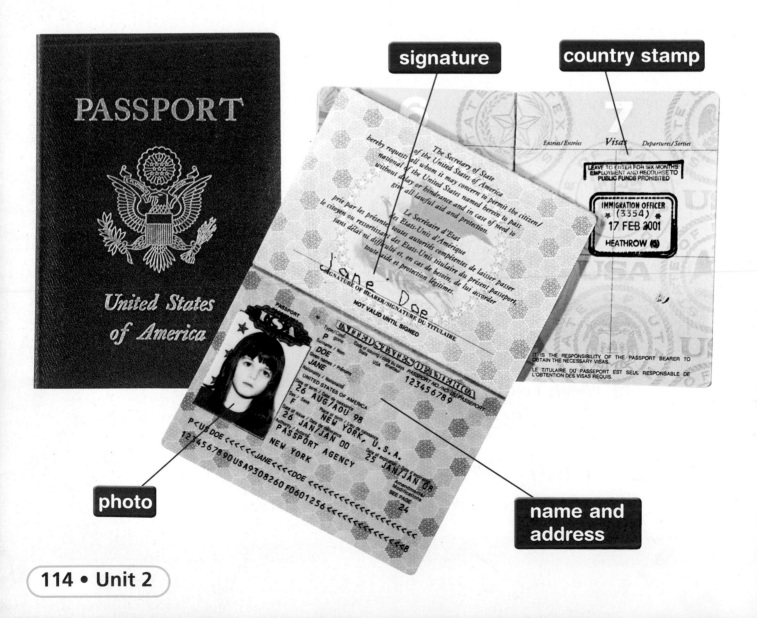

signature

country stamp

photo

name and address

You can make believe you have a passport.

Step 1 Fold a piece of paper in half.
Write **My Passport** on the cover.

Step 2 Draw a picture of your face on
the inside.

Step 3 Write your name, address, and
the country where you live.

**Which country would
you like to visit with
your passport?**

Eric Benson
321 Verde Street
Sunnyville, AZ
85555
U.S.A.

Core Lesson 7

Vocabulary
neighbors

Reading Skill
Compare and Contrast

Our Country's Neighbors

Build on What You Know

The United States has two countries that are near it. The people of those countries are like people who live near you.

Canada and Mexico

Canada and Mexico are neighbors of our country. **Neighbors** are people who live near each other. Canada is the neighbor to the north. Mexico is the neighbor to the south.

main idea

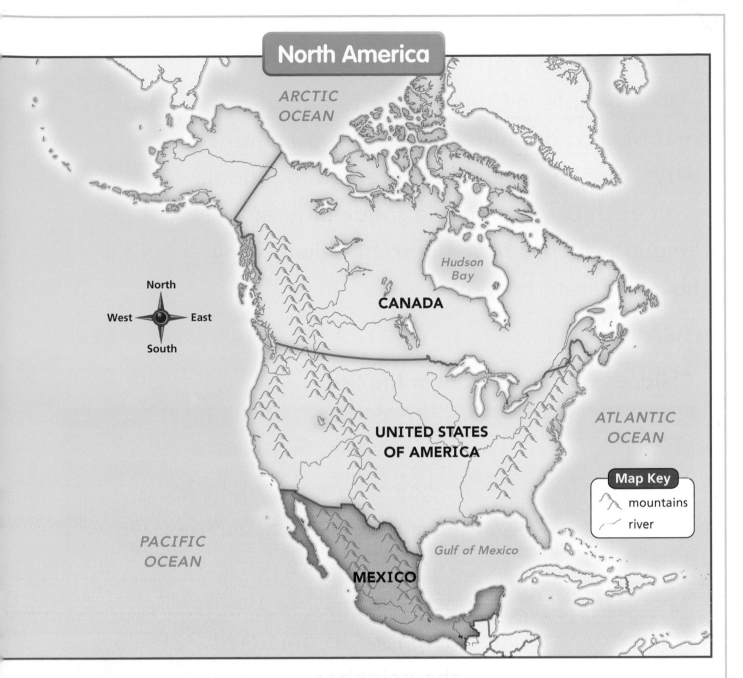

North America

ARCTIC OCEAN

Hudson Bay

CANADA

North
West • East
South

UNITED STATES OF AMERICA

ATLANTIC OCEAN

Map Key
⋀ mountains
∿ river

PACIFIC OCEAN

Gulf of Mexico

MEXICO

Skill **Reading Maps** What kind of land is found in all three countries shown on this map?

Review How are Canada, the United States, and Mexico alike?

People Are Alike and Different

main ★ idea

The people in Canada, the United States, and Mexico are alike and different in many ways. They have jobs. Children go to school.

In each country people speak different languages. They have different beliefs. They have different holidays.

Children read at school in Mexico.

Children have a birthday party in the United States.

Children play hockey in Canada.

Review In what ways are people in the three countries alike?

Lesson Review

❶ **Vocabulary** Write something you know about our country's **neighbors.**

❷ **Main Idea** In what ways are the people of Canada, the United States, and Mexico different?

 Activity Draw a map of North America. Write Canada, the United States, and Mexico on your map.

Primary Sources

Flags and Holidays

Did you know that every country has its own flag? People celebrate their country's birthday with flags and parades. In Canada, Mexico, and the United States, people wear colors of their flag.

Canada Day is on July 1 each year.

Mexican Independence is celebrated on September 15 and 16.

Independence Day in the United States is on July 4.

Activities

1. **Tell About It** Compare the flags of Canada, Mexico, and the United States.

2. **Draw It** Draw pictures or tell about ways your family celebrates Independence Day.

Visit Education Place for more primary sources. www.eduplace.com/kids/hmss05/

Big Idea

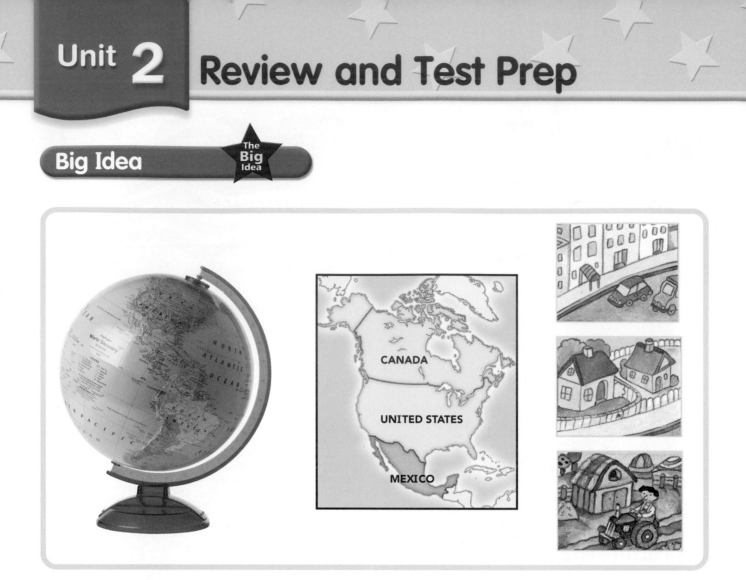

Use the chart to answer the questions.

1. What does a globe show? (page 74)

2. What continent do we live on? (page 76)

3. A country has _____, towns, and farms. (page 102)

Facts and Main Ideas

4. What kinds of land are on Earth? (page 82)

5. What kinds of water are on Earth? (page 84)

6. In what ways do seasons and weather change how people live? (page 98)

Vocabulary

Write the letter or word for each correct answer.

7. Africa is a _____ .

8. Trees are a _____ .

9. A _____ is a time of the year.

10. An _____ is a large body of salty water.

> **A. season** (page 97)
>
> **B. state** (page 110)
>
> **C. continent** (page 76)
>
> **D. ocean** (page 75)
>
> **E. natural resource** (page 88)

✔ **Test Practice**

11. What does the word **citizen** mean?

   A. A place with many people living in it

   B. A person who belongs to a state or a country

   C. A place that is hot and wet in summer

   D. Another name for a continent

Critical Thinking

Cause and Effect

12. Why do people try to save water and trees?

13. What makes cities grow bigger and bigger?

Skillbuilders

Compare Globes and Maps

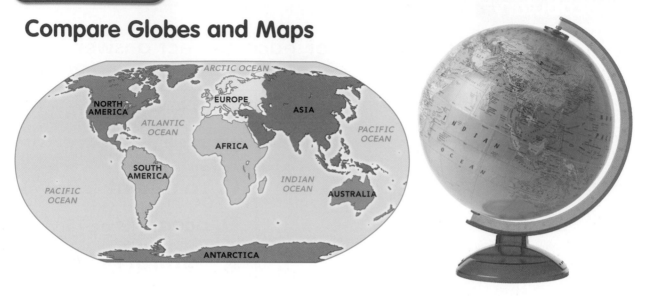

14. Find a continent on the globe and on the map. What is its name?

15. What ocean is near the North Pole?

Find Near and Far

16. Is the rabbit near the house or far from it?

17. The tree is _____ from the house.

Unit Activity ★ The Big Idea

Global Address Envelope

Your global address is where you live in the world.

❶ Fold a big sheet of paper in half to make the envelope.

❷ Write your name, street, town, state, country, world.

❸ Make a stamp.

Kim Lee
21 Green Street
Atlanta, Georgia
United States
Earth

Current Events

Make a poster of **Places in the News**. Find current events from Weekly Reader on the social studies website.

Places In The News

New York City

💻 **Technology**
Current Events Project
www.eduplace.com/kids/hmss05/

In Your Classroom

Look for these Social Studies Independent Books in your classroom.

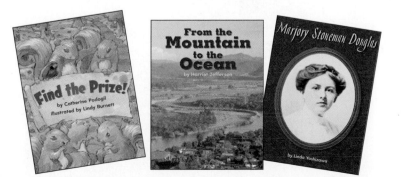

Find the Prize!
by Catherine Podojil
illustrated by Lindy Burnett

From the Mountain to the Ocean
by Harriet Jefferson

Marjory Stoneman Douglas
by Linda Yoshizawa

At the Library

Look for these books at your library.

A Cool Drink of Water
by Barbara Kerley

Map and Map Making
by Barbara Taylor

UNIT 3

World of Work

Everything costs money,
Nothing is free today;
So save your dimes
and pennies—
You always have to pay.

—From "You Always Have to Pay"
by Lois Lenski

The Big Idea

What choices do
people make to get
the things they want?

Vocabulary Preview

goods

Goods are things we buy or use. A supermarket sells many goods like vegetables and fruit.

page 139

services

The post office has many mail **services.**

page 139

Reading Strategy

Monitor and Clarify Use the monitor and clarify strategy in Lessons 1,2, and 3.
Summarize Use the summarize strategy in Lessons 4 and 5.

save

Many children **save** money for things they want. page 147

factory

A **factory** is a building where workers use machines to make goods. Toys are made in a factory. page 154

Needs and Wants

▶ **Vocabulary**
needs
scarcity
wants

Reading Skill
Compare and Contrast

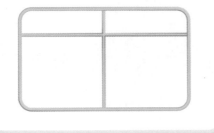

Build on What You Know

Every person needs food. What is your favorite food?

Needs

Needs are things we must have to live. We need food, clothing, and shelter. People work to earn money. They use money to buy what they need. Families do not always have enough money to buy all they want. That is called **scarcity.**

main idea ⭐

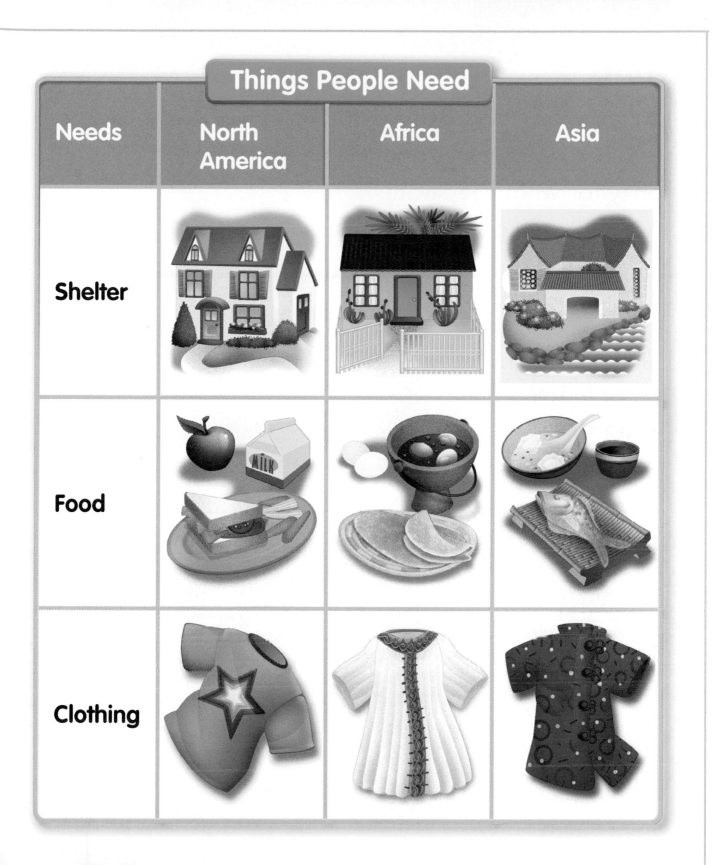

Things People Need

Needs	North America	Africa	Asia
Shelter			
Food			
Clothing			

Review Why do people work to get money?

Wants

Wants are things we would like to have. Families make choices about how to spend money for what they want.

Help Jill make a choice about what to buy.

Jill has one dollar saved in her bank.

She wants to get another fish for her fishbowl.

$1.00

Today she saw a book she wants.

My First Year

$2.00

Look at the prices of the fish and the book. What can Jill do with her money?

Review What choice would you make and why?

Lesson Review

❶ Vocabulary Name two **needs** that families have.

❷ Main Idea Why do families have to make choices about ways to spend money?

Activity Write a story about a choice you made when you had money to spend.

A Scarcity of Scissors

CAST

Narrator	Andy	Maria
Ms. Lee	Lan	Deb

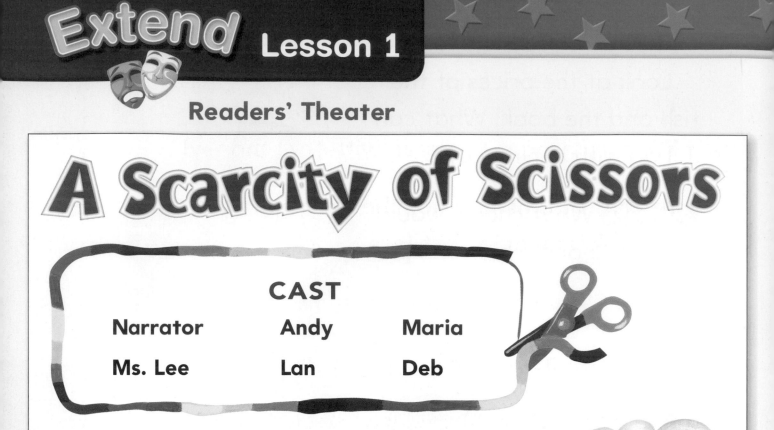

Narrator: Ms. Lee looked sad one day. She told her class, "I'm sorry to say—"

Ms. Lee: I counted scissors and I found there aren't enough to go around.

Deb: Let's share the scissors! That will do! I cut first, then Lan cuts, too.

Lan: But if we share, I have to wait. My art work will be very late.

Andy: There's money in our Class Fund. Let's buy scissors for everyone.

Maria: If that's a joke, it isn't funny. We're buying a hamster with that money!

Andy: A hamster's not the only pet. A goldfish would cost less to get.

Deb: Or we can save a little more!

Lan: And as we save, I guess we'll share.

Ms. Lee: We still have scarcity today. But we've worked out our problem. Hooray! Hooray!

Activities

1. **Talk About It** Talk with a partner. Think of another way Ms. Lee's class could solve their problem.

2. **Make It** Make a comic strip to retell this story.

Make a Decision

▶ **Vocabulary**
decision

When people make a **decision,** they make choices.

Learn the Skill

Look at the picture. Read the steps and make a decision.

Step 1 Think about what is happening. Two children want to eat pie. There is only one slice of pie.

Step 2 Tell what the choices are.

- One child can eat the pie.

- The children can share the pie.

- No one can eat the pie.

Step 3 Think about each choice. Is it good for everyone? Decide on the best choice.

Practice the Skill

Look at the picture below and read the words. Help the boys decide what to do.

1 Think about what the boys could do. List the choices.

2 Think about each choice. Is the choice good for everyone?

3 Decide on the best choice. Tell why you think it is a good decision.

Can I play?

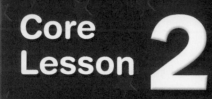

Core Lesson 2

Goods and Services

Vocabulary
sell
goods
services
volunteers

Reading Skill
Classify

Build on What You know
You have been to a store where there are things to buy and people to help you.

Making Money
People work to earn money to buy things. People also sell things to get money. To **sell** means to give things for money.

main idea ⭐

GAS

Fruit & Vegetables

HAR

Goods and Services

Food, books, homes, cars, and shoes are goods. **Goods** are the things we buy or use. People may sell goods to make money.

A dentist and a taxi driver earn money for the services they do. **Services** are jobs people do to help others. People work to buy goods and get services. **Volunteers** are people who help others for no money. Can you name the goods and the services in the picture below?

Review What are two ways people can earn money to buy things they need?

Community Goods and Services

In your community there are places where you can get goods and services. Look at the chart on this page. It shows places where people get goods and services.

main idea

Goods	Services
Stores	Doctor's Office
Bakery	Library
Flower Shop	Hospital
Farm	Post Office
Gas Station	Town Hall
Yard Sale	Fire Station

Goods and Services Jobs

Some people have jobs making goods. Other people have service jobs. A mail carrier does a service job. Look at the children selling lemonade. Is this job selling goods or services?

main idea

Review What are places where you get goods and services?

Lesson Review

❶ **Vocabulary** Make a list of **goods** you use every day.

❷ **Main Idea** What is the difference between goods and services?

HANDS ON **Activity** Draw a picture of someone who works in a service job.

Biography

Thanh Lam

Thanh Lam of Honolulu, Hawaii, is a very successful business owner. In 2002 he won an award for being the best small business owner.

Thanh came to the United States from Vietnam with little money. He opened a sandwich shop. People in Honolulu loved the bread he baked. Soon Thanh was selling his goods to airlines and hotels.

A harbor in Vietnam.

HAWAII

VIETNAM

Mr. Lam says to his workers, "Try to do your best. Work hard. Be honest and keep your word."

Activities

1. **Think About It** Why do you think Thanh Lam had courage to start his own business?

2. **Write About It** Write about a job that you would like to have.

 Technology Read more biographies on www.eduplace.com/kids/hmss05/

143

Buy, Trade, and Save

▶ **Vocabulary**
cost
save

◎ **Reading Skill**
Main Idea and Details

Build on What You Know

When you are ready to buy something, you find out how much money you have to spend.

Buying

When your family shops, they look at the cost of things. The **cost** is how much money is needed to buy something. People make buying choices by looking at the cost of the things they want to buy.

main idea (★)

Trading

Sometimes people trade goods and services to get things they want. In school, you may like your friend's cookies and she likes your popcorn. You could trade the popcorn for the cookies.

Review Do you think it is better to buy things or trade things? Why?

I will dry the dishes for you today.

These children trade chores.

Making Choices

Families have to make choices about what they can buy. Tina's parents want a new car because they have a new baby. Her family also wants to take a big summer vacation. Here are some things they talked about.

- They do not have money for both.
- Their car is too small and it is old.
- They can have a short vacation, but they want a longer vacation.

They chose to buy a new car. Why do you think they made that choice?

Saving Money

People often save money to buy things they want. To **save** means to put away and keep. People can save money in a bank. The bank is a safe place to keep money.

Review Why is it important to save money?

Lesson Review

1 **Vocabulary** Tell one way that you can **save** money.

2 **Main Idea** Why do people make choices when they want to buy something?

HANDS ON **Activity** Make a shopping list of 3 things that you want to buy. You can draw pictures or write words. Write down how much you think each thing costs.

Economics

A Doggy Bank

You can save money. Make a bank and watch your money add up!

Use a plastic milk or juice container with a cap.

Step 1

Make the container into a doggy bank. Add eyes, ears, a mouth, a tail, and some feet.

Step 2

Have your teacher cut a slot for coins and bills.

Step 3

Start putting your coins in the bank today!

Read a Graph

▶ **Vocabulary**
picture graph

People compare costs before they buy things. A **picture graph** is a chart that can help you compare things.

Learn the Skill

This graph compares the costs of foods.

Step 1 Each picture of a dollar stands for one dollar. Count the dollar bills under the milk. It costs two dollars to buy the milk.

Step 2 There are three dollar bills under the orange juice. The orange juice costs three dollars. It costs more than the milk.

Step 3 There is one dollar bill under the bananas. They cost one dollar. They cost less than the milk.

Look at the graph below to compare costs.
Then follow the directions.

1 Which costs more, the eggs or the bread?

2 Which costs less, the cereal or the orange juice?

3 How much would it cost to buy milk and cereal? Count to find out.

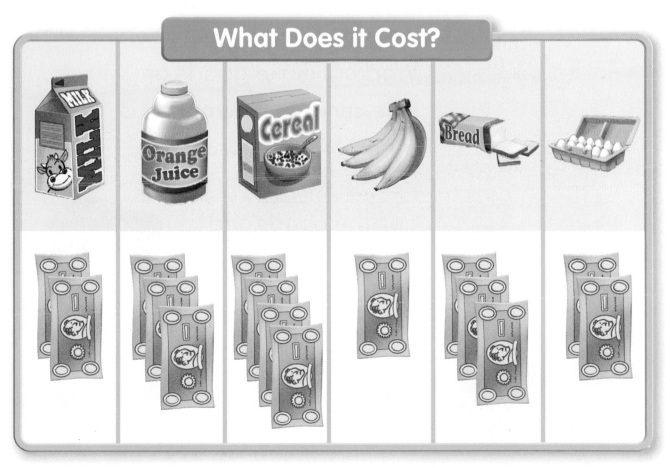

What Does it Cost?

All Kinds of Jobs

Build on What You Know

Think about the jobs of people you know.

Why People Have Jobs

Most adults have jobs. They work in offices or schools. They work at home or outdoors. Workers make goods or give services. A **worker** is a person who does a job. People work to get the goods and services they want.

Vocabulary
worker
factory

Reading Skill
Cause and
Effect

main
(★)
idea

Mr. Chong is a mail carrier. He is paid money each week for his work. This shows what Mr. Chong did with his money this week.

Review What services do people buy?

Jobs at a Factory

This bread factory has many workers. A **factory** is a place where workers use machines to make goods. Some workers make the bread. Others put the bread in bags. The factory workers are paid for their work. Everyone's job is important.

Review Who are people who make goods?

Lesson Review

❶ Vocabulary Use the words **factory** and **worker** in a sentence.

❷ Main Idea What do people do to earn money to buy goods and services?

HANDS ON **Activity** Draw a picture of a toy factory.

Sarah Chang

Sarah Chang was only four years old when she began to play the violin. At five years old, she was playing in concerts! Sarah Chang is now one of the best violinists in the world.

Fernando Bujones

When he was young, Fernando Bujones (Boo-hoh-nayz) was not very strong. A visit to a doctor changed his life. One day a doctor told Fernando's mother that dance lessons would make him stronger. Fernando Bujones has worked as a famous ballet dancer and a teacher.

Activities

1. **Talk About It** Tell about the responsibilities you would have in a job.

2. **Draw It** Draw a picture of you as a worker.

Technology Read more biographies. www.eduplace.com/kids/hmss05/

Getting Food to Market

Vocabulary

machine

seller

buyer

Reading Skill

Sequence

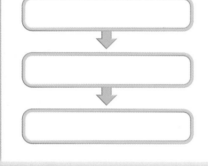

Build on What You Know

Did you ever wonder where orange juice comes from?

Getting Food from Other Places

Some food we eat is grown far away from where we live. People grow food and send it to other states and even to other countries.

(★) main idea

Look at the map. Most of the oranges and orange juice in the United States come from California and Florida.

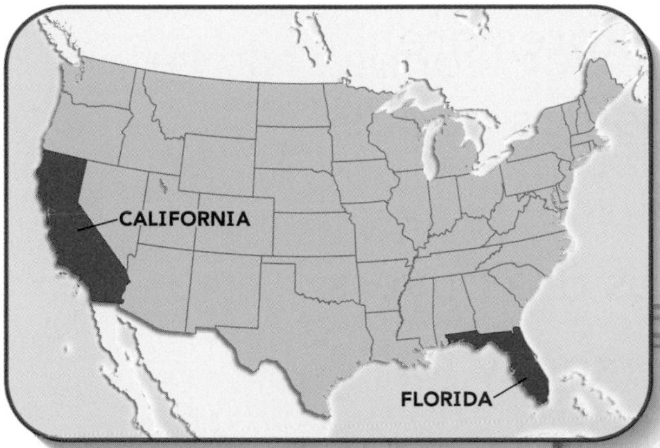

CALIFORNIA

FLORIDA

Review Why do you think people want some food that is grown in other places?

From Tree to Table

It takes many workers and machines to get orange juice ready to drink. A **machine** is an object that does work for people.

main idea

When orange juice is ready, it is sent to stores. People who work at stores are sellers. A **seller** is someone who has goods and services that others can buy.

People who shop in the stores are buyers. A **buyer** is someone who pays money for goods or services.

1 **Pick the oranges.**

2 **Squeeze the juice.**

4 **Sell the juice.**

3 **Put juice into containers.**

Review Who are the buyers and sellers of orange juice at the store?

Lesson Review

1 **Vocabulary** Tell what a **machine** is.

2 **Main Idea** What steps does it take to get orange juice to homes?

Activity Draw a picture chart that shows how orange juice is made. Write sentences to go with your chart.

Stone Soup
A folktale from Europe

Once upon a time, there was a long dry spell. The people of one village didn't have much food. A young girl solved the problem of scarcity for that day's meal.

"Let's make stone soup!" said the girl. "All we need is a big pot of water and wood for a fire."

Some people brought a little water. Others brought logs for the fire.

"Here I have a stone from the river," the girl said. Plop! She dropped the stone into the pot.

The water boiled. "This smells good," the girl said. "But it would be even better with a few onions."

A few people ran home. They came back with onions for the pot.

The water boiled. "This smells just right," the girl said. "But it would be even better if we had some carrots."

More people ran home. Each one came back with a carrot or two for the pot.

The girl stirred the soup. "This soup is almost done," she said. "If we just had some noodles..."

Three or four people ran off. Soon they came back with noodles for the pot.

The soup boiled. The girl served stone soup to everyone. When they had eaten the last drop, the girl plucked the stone from the pot. She wiped it off, and put it in her pocket.

"Tomorrow," she said, "we can make stone stew!"

Activities

1. **Think About It** What is the main idea of the story?

2. **Write It** Write a recipe for stone soup.

Use a Compass Rose

Map and Globe Skills

▶ **Vocabulary**

compass rose

People use maps to find directions to places they go. The **compass rose** on a map shows four directions: north, south, east, and west.

Learn the Skill

Look at the globe. Put your finger on the **X** before reading each step.

Step 1 North is the direction going towards the North Pole. Move your finger north from the **X**.

Step 2 South is the direction toward the South Pole. Move your finger south from the **X**.

Step 3 When you are facing north, places to the right are east. Places to the left are west. Move your finger east and west from the **X**.

North Pole

South Pole

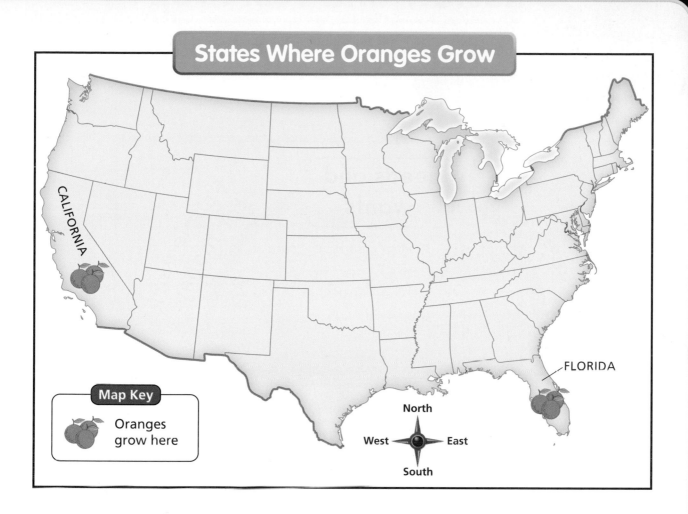

States Where Oranges Grow

CALIFORNIA

FLORIDA

Map Key

Oranges grow here

North

West —•— East

South

Practice the Skill

Look at the map and follow the directions.

1 Find the compass rose. Start at the oranges in Florida. Use your finger and show where north is.

2 Now put your finger on California. Move your finger to show the direction east.

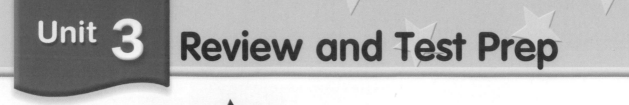

Unit 3 Review and Test Prep

Big Idea

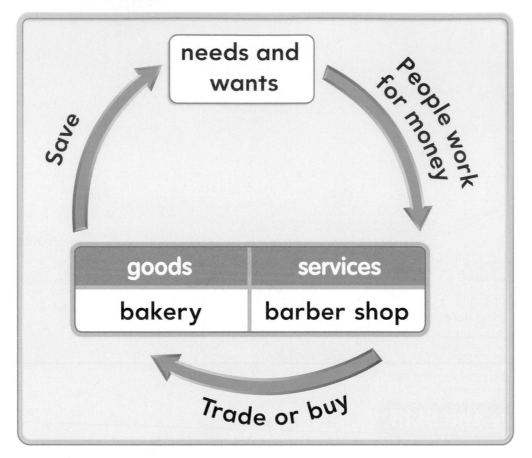

Answer these questions.

1. People work to earn _____. (page 130)

2. What are some goods and services? (page 139)

3. What are three things all people need? (page 130)

Facts and Main Ideas

4. Why are people not able to buy everything they need? (page 130)

5. Why do people save money? (page 147)

Vocabulary

Write the letter or word for each answer.

6. People who do not get paid for the work they do

7. A place where people make goods

8. To put away and keep

9. Someone who pays money to get goods and services

A. factory (page 154)

B. volunteers (page 139)

C. buyer (page 160)

D. scarcity (page 130)

E. save (page 147)

✔ Test Practice

10. What does the word **scarcity** mean?

   A. Having a lot of goods

   B. Things people buy and sell

   C. Not having enough of something

   D. A kind of service job people have

Critical Thinking

Compare and Contrast

11. What is the same and different about saving and spending?

12. What is the same and different about buying and trading things?

Skillbuilders

Read a Picture Graph

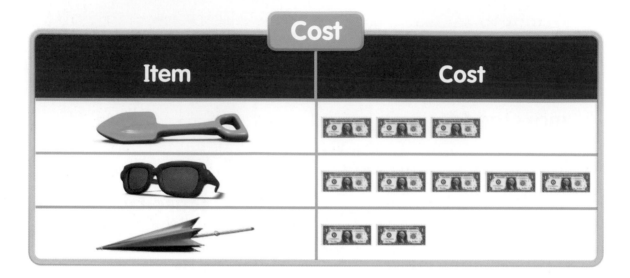

Item	Cost
(shovel)	🖼️🖼️🖼️
(sunglasses)	🖼️🖼️🖼️🖼️🖼️
(umbrella)	🖼️🖼️

13. Which item costs the most money?

14. How much would it cost to buy the sunglasses and the shovel?

15. If you had five dollars, what could you buy?

Use a Compass Rose

This map shows Jenny's neighborhood.

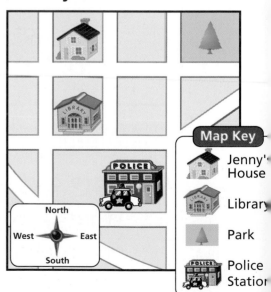

Map Key

Jenny's House

Library

Park

Police Station

16. What direction does Jenny walk from her house to the library?

17. What is south of the library?

18. What is north of the library?

Unit Activity

The Big Idea

Make Trading Cards

Make two sets of trading cards. Show goods on one set of cards and services on the other.

❶ Place the stack face down and take turns drawing cards.

❷ Trade goods cards for services cards.

Current Events Project

Make a **Service Jobs** chart. Find current events from Weekly Reader on the social studies website.

> Services
> dentist
> barber
> mail carrier

Technology
Current Events Project
www.eduplace.com/kids/hmss05/

In Your Classroom

Look for these Social Studies Independent Books in your classroom.

A Job for You
by Diane Moses
illustrated by Shirley Beckes

Walt Disney's World
by Marjorie Miller

The Life of a Dollar Bill
by Chris Anderson
illustrated by Alan Flinn

At the Library

Look for these books at your library.

Bread Is for Eating
by David and Phillis Gershator

Follow the Money
by Loreen Leedy

UNIT 4

Everything Changes

The days gone by—
What shall I tell you,
My grandchildren,
Of the days gone by?

—From "Spell Song"
A Kwakiutl song

The Big Idea

In what ways do people and things change over time?

Vocabulary Preview

Technology
e • glossary
e • word games
www.eduplace.com/kids/hmss05/

history

History is the story of people and things from the past. page 177

settler

A **settler** is someone who comes to live in a new place. page 191

Reading Strategy

Monitor and Clarify Use the monitor and clarify strategy in Lessons 1, 2, 3, and 4.
Summarize Use the summarize strategy in Lessons 5 and 6.

transportation

Transportation is a way to move people and things from place to place. A train is one kind of transportation. page 208

communication

Communication is a way people share news and ideas. A phone call is one kind of communication. page 216

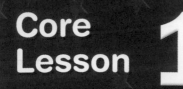

Learning About the Past

Vocabulary

present

past

history

future

Reading Skill

Compare and Contrast

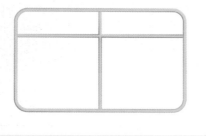

Build on What You Know

Think of something fun you did last summer. That fun time happened before today.

Past and Present

The **present** is what is happening today. The **past** is what happened before today. What is something you can do now that you could not do in the past?

main (★) *idea*

In the past you were smaller. In the present you are getting taller.

A Story of the Past

History tells a story of the past. Your family has a history. Here are three ways to find out about the past.

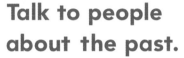

Talk to people about the past.

Read books or listen to stories about the past.

Look at real things and pictures from the past.

Review What can you do to find out about your family history?

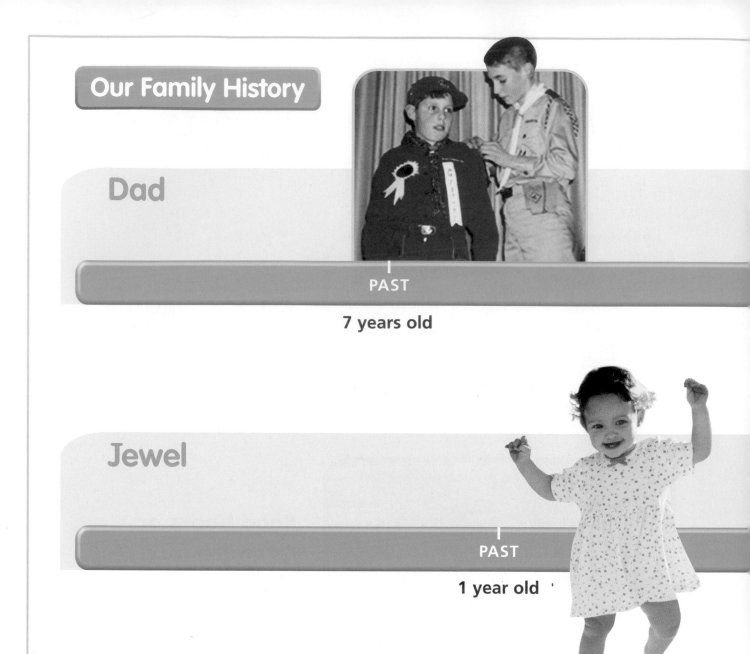

Dad

PAST

7 years old

Jewel

PAST

1 year old

Future

The **future** is the time after today. Tomorrow, next week, and next year are all in the future. In the future you will get bigger and go on to other schools.

main idea (★)

PRESENT

FUTURE

35 years old

65 years old

PRESENT

FUTURE

7 years old

25 years old

Review What things can happen in your class in the future?

Lesson Review

❶ Vocabulary Use the words **past, present,** and **future** in sentences.

❷ Main Idea What is history?

HANDS ON **Activity** Draw a picture that shows something you might do in the future.

179

Family History Day

Cast

Narrator	Sam
Alicia	Liz

Narrator: Today is Family History Day at school. Some of us brought things from our families.

Alicia: I have this old picture. It is my grandpa's first car. That's my grandpa when he was young.

Sam: I have this old bank. My mom had it when she was seven. You put money in the elephant's trunk. Then the elephant throws it into the bank.

Liz: This is an old puppet my grandma had.

Narrator: What could you bring to Family History Day?

Activities

1. **Draw It** Draw a picture of something you could bring to Family History Day.

2. **Act It Out** Use your drawing to tell about your family's history.

Use a Timeline

A **timeline** shows when things happened. It shows what happened first, next, and last.

▶ **Vocabulary**
timeline

Learn the Skill

Step 1 This timeline shows Marco's week at school. The week started on Monday. It ended on Friday.

Step 2 Read what Marco did on each day of the week. Start at the beginning of the week, Monday.

Step 3 Tell what Marco did on Monday, Tuesday, and Wednesday. Use the words **first**, **next**, and **last** to tell when things happened.

Monday

I planted seeds.

Look at the timeline again. Then follow the directions.

1 Tell what Marco did on Thursday and Friday. Use the words **first** and **last** to tell the order that things happened.

2 Tell about each thing that happened between Wednesday and Friday. Use the words **first**, **next**, and **last**.

Marco's Week at School

Tuesday	Wednesday	Thursday	Friday
I fed the pet.	I read a book.	I wrote a letter.	I played on the swings.

The First Americans

Vocabulary

American
    Indians

Reading Skill
Classify

Build on What You Know

Do you know who were the first people to live in your community?

The First People

American Indians were the first people to live in North America. Hundreds of years ago, more than one thousand groups of American Indians lived all over North America. Two groups are the Chumash and the Cherokee.

Cherokee

(Review) Who were the first people to live in our country?

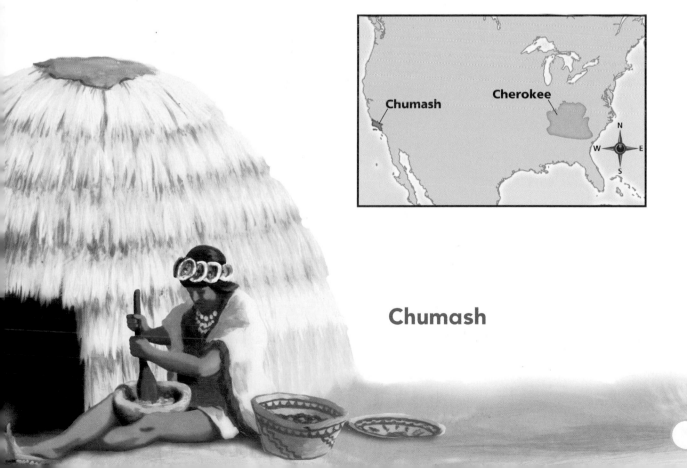

Chumash

The Chumash

Chumash men and women made many main idea ★ things. They built canoes to catch fish for food and to get from place to place. Women made baskets from grasses. Some Chumash painted pictures in caves. The cave paintings are still important to the Chumash today.

Chumash paintings in a cave near Santa Barbara, California

The Cherokee

The Cherokee did the Eagle Dance to welcome important visitors from other places. Today, some Cherokee still **main idea ★** do the Eagle Dance on special days. The dance helps them remember what life was like in the past.

(Review) What do the Cherokee and the Chumash still enjoy from the past?

Cherokee Eagle Dancer

Lesson Review

❶ **Vocabulary** Tell something you know about **American Indians.**

❷ **Main Idea** What did the Chumash make and use in the past?

HANDS ON **Activity** Draw pictures of things the Chumash made long ago.

Literature

Moon of Falling Leaves

This poem about trees in autumn is told by Cherokee people.

Long ago, the trees were told
they must stay awake
seven days and nights,
but only the cedar,
the pine and the spruce
stayed awake until
that seventh night.
The reward they were given
was to always be green,
while all the other trees
must shed their leaves.

So, each autumn, the leaves
of the sleeping trees fall.
They cover the floor
of our woodlands with colors
as bright as the flowers
that come with the spring.
The leaves return the strength
of one more year's growth
to the earth.

This journey
the leaves are taking
is part of that great circle
which holds us all close to the earth.

Activities

1. **Think About It** Why do you think Cherokee people share stories and poems?

2. **Write It** Write a sentence that tells what the weather in fall is like where you live.

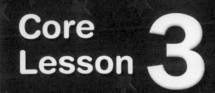

Family Life, Past and Present

Build on What You Know

Think about moving to a new place. What problems can you have when you move?

New Families Arrive

American Indians were the first people living in North America. Then people from Europe came to trade and fish. Soon families from Europe came here to live.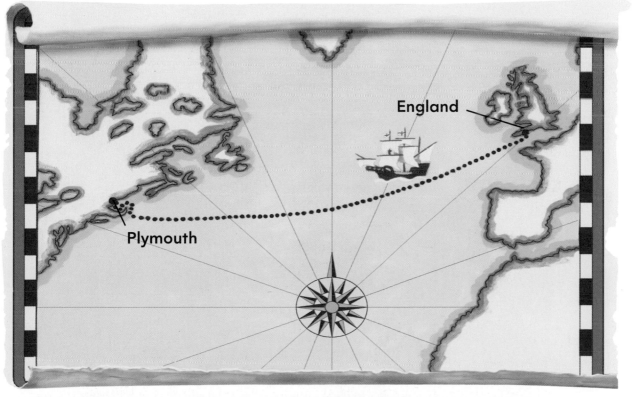

main idea ⭐

The Pilgrims were settlers who came from the country of England. **Settlers** are people who come to live in a new place. The Pilgrims came to be free to practice their beliefs in God. The Pilgrims met the Wampanoag who were living on the land.

Review Where did the Pilgrims come from?

England

Plymouth

The Pilgrims sailed on the Mayflower in 1620.

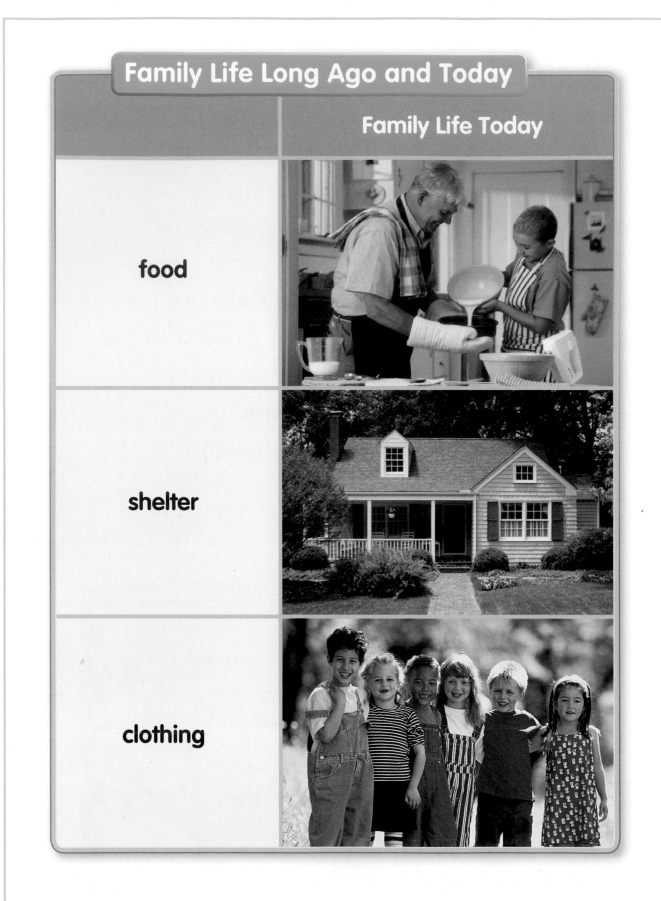

Family Life Long Ago and Today

	Family Life Today
food	
shelter	
clothing	

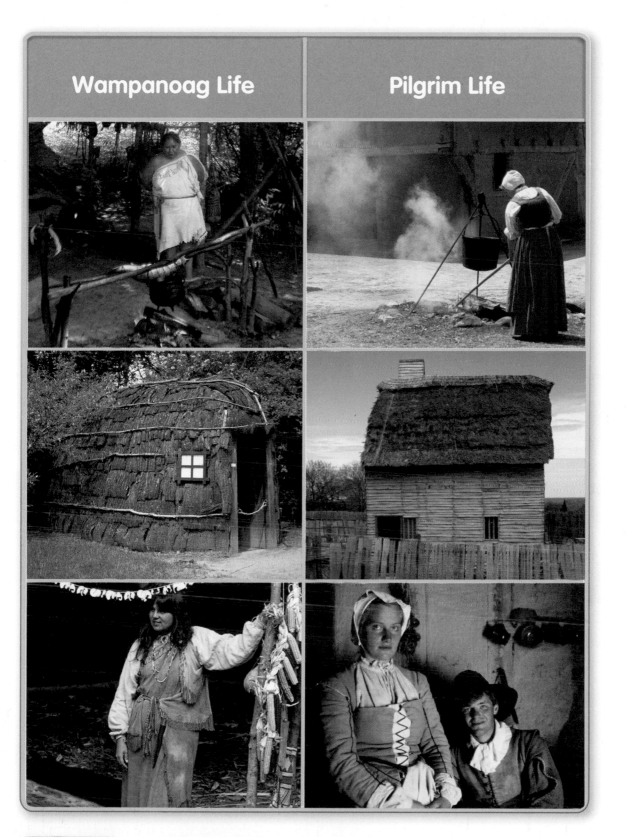

| Wampanoag Life | Pilgrim Life |

Review In what ways is family life today the same or different from the past?

Making a New Life

The first winter was very hard for the Pilgrims. There was not enough food and it was very cold. Many people got sick. In the spring, the Wampanoag showed the Pilgrims how to grow food. Everyone worked hard. Women took care of the home. Men farmed and hunted. Children helped their parents.

main idea ★

Celebrating the Harvest

In the fall, the Pilgrims had enough food to eat. They had a big harvest celebration. The **harvest** is the crops that are ready to be gathered. Many Wampanoag shared the harvest celebration. Today, we call our harvest celebration Thanksgiving.

main idea (★)

Review Why do you think the Pilgrims had a harvest celebration?

Lesson Review

❶ **Vocabulary** Tell what a **settler** is.

❷ **Main Idea** Why was the first winter hard for the Pilgrims?

HANDS ON **Activity** Make a chart that shows how life for Pilgrims was different from your family's life today.

From the book

Tattered Sails

by Verla Kay

The family in this story left England about 300 years ago. They moved to this country to make a better life.

One room cabin,
Rush beds, soft.
Greased cloth windows,
Ladder, loft.

Mother resting,
Baby born.
Local natives,
Sharing corn.

Thomas, Edward,
Mary Jane,
Carting water,
Planting grain.

Activities

1. **Write About It** Write a sentence that tells how your life is different from the lives of the children in the story.

2. **Read About It** Find Tattered Sails at the library.

Solve a Conflict

▶ **Vocabulary**
conflict

A **conflict** happens when people do not agree. Families can find ways to agree.

Learn the Skill

Follow the steps to solve a conflict.

Step 1 One child wants to go to the toy store. The other wants to go to the pet store. Tell what the conflict is.

Step 2 Think of some ways the family could help to solve the conflict.

- Go to the toy store today and the pet store tomorrow.

- Go to both stores today.

Step 3 Which way would you choose?

Practice the Skill

Look at the picture below. Read the words. Then follow the directions.

1. Tell what the conflict is.
2. Think of some ways to try to solve the conflict.
3. Choose one way to solve the conflict. Tell why it is a good way.

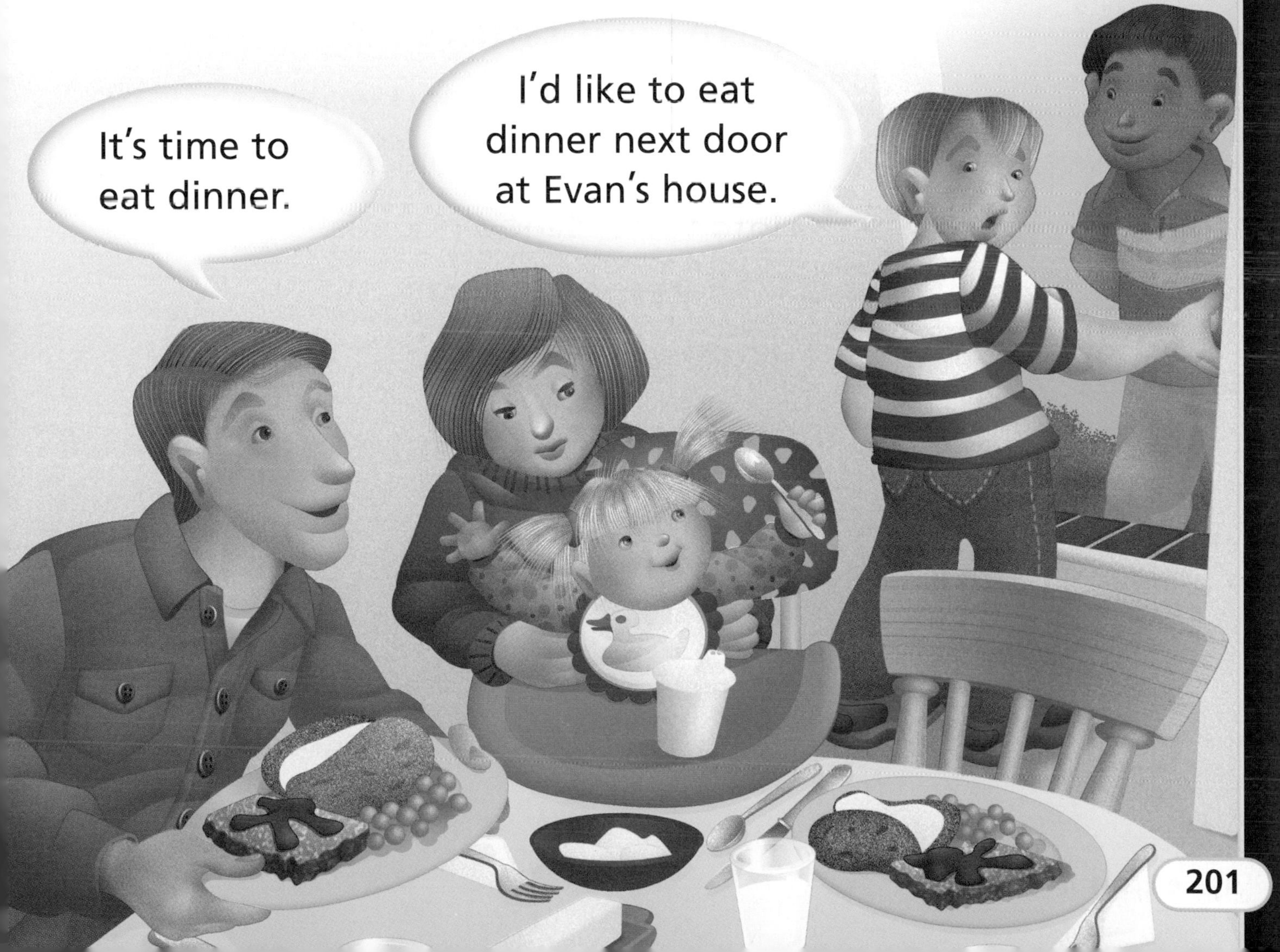

It's time to eat dinner.
I'd like to eat dinner next door at Evan's house.

▶ **Vocabulary**
education

◎ **Reading Skill**
**Compare and
Contrast**

Going to School Long Ago

Build on What You Know

What things in your classroom help you to learn?

A School in One Room

The first settlers taught their children to read and write at home. Later, people built one-room schoolhouses. Children of all ages learned together.

main idea (★)

Review How are your school and the old schoolhouse alike and different?

School Tools

In the past, children used different tools main idea to help them learn. They wrote on small chalkboards called slates. Sometimes they wrote with pens made from feathers with metal tips.

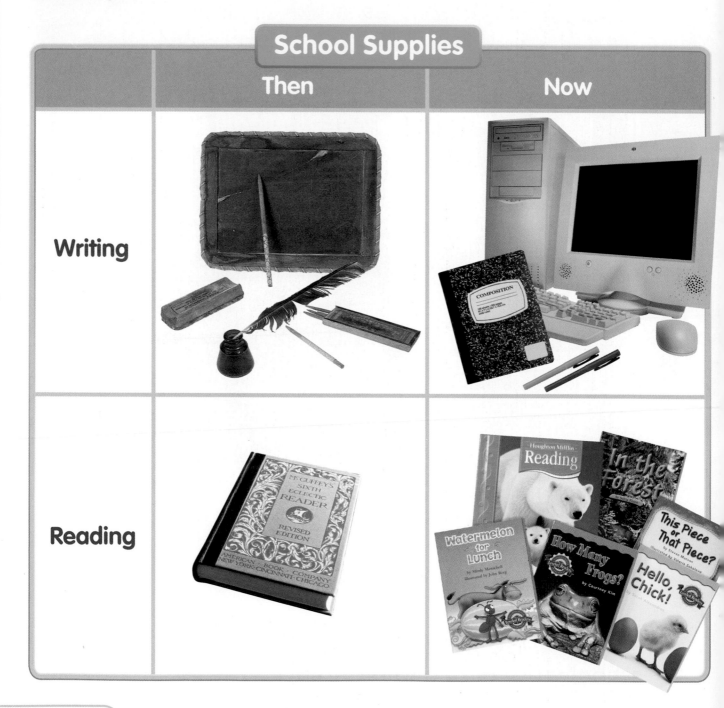

School Supplies

	Then	Now
Writing		
Reading		

School Today

Today, most children in the United States go to school to get an education. **Education** is all the things people learn, such as math, history, and reading.

main idea ⭐

Review How are things at your school different than in the past?

Lesson Review

❶ **Vocabulary** What does **education** mean?

❷ **Main Idea** What do you think it was like at school long ago?

HANDS ON **Activity** Draw pictures of things in a child's classroom in the past.

Hornbooks

What does a cow's horn have to do with reading?

Long ago, children learned to read using a hornbook. Paper cost a lot of money then. So people made hornbooks.

First, they cut a wooden board.

Next, they glued a written paper onto the board.

Last, they covered the paper with a thin piece of cow's horn.

A gingerbread hornbook was a fun way to learn the alphabet. Each time children learned a letter they got to eat it!

Activities

1. Draw It Draw a chart that shows the steps to make a hornbook.

2. Make It Write the alphabet to make your own hornbook.

 Technology Learn about other primary sources at Education Place. www.eduplace.com/kids/hmss05/

Moving People and Things

Build on What You Know

Did you ride the bus to school today? A bus is one way to move from home to school.

Transportation

Long ago, people walked or rode on animals to get around. Transportation was very slow then. **Transportation** is the way we move people and things.

main idea (★)

Inventions

People made inventions because they wanted better transportation. An **invention** is a new tool or way of doing something. Trains, cars, and airplanes were all inventions at one time. Some inventions make moving people and things faster and easier.

(★) main idea

Orville and Wilbur Wright invented an airplane.

Review Why do you think people make inventions?

Steamboats traveled on rivers from city to city.

Steam engines were the start of railroads.

Transportation Changes

Transportation keeps changing. *main ★ idea*
Trains, planes, and high speed boats help people to travel anywhere on Earth. It takes less time to move people and things than ever before.

Review How do transportation inventions change the way people live?

Cars made travel easier for many people.

Now it is possible to travel into space.

Lesson Review

1 Vocabulary Use the word **invention** in a sentence about transportation.

2 Main Idea In what ways is transportation today different than in the past?

HANDS ON **Activity** Draw the kinds of transportation you use.

Rush Hour

by Christine Loomis

Do you hurry to get to school? That is a busy rush hour for you.

Engines start up with a jerk.
People hurry off to work.

Horns go beep-beep, whistles blow,
Planes go fast,
Trucks go slow.

Trolleys sway, ferries rock,
Time keeps ticking
On the clock.

Cars on side streets,
Trains on tracks,
Whizzing,
Zipping,
Clicky
Clack,
Rumbling,
Roaring,
Jiggling,
Jumping,
Left turn,
Right turn,
Backing,
Bumping.

Activities

1. **Talk About It** Tell about a rush hour at your school.

2. **Write It** Make a list of the kinds of transportation in the poem.

Compare Points of View

▶ **Vocabulary**
point of view

A **point of view** is what someone thinks. People can have different points of view about transportation.

Learn the Skill

Step 1 Gus has an idea about the best way to get to school. Read what he thinks.

Step 2 Gus thinks that the bus is the best way to get to school. That is Gus's point of view.

Step 3 Gus has a reason for his point of view. He likes to be with his friends on the bus.

Gus

The bus is the best way to get to school. I can be with my friends on the bus.

Practice the Skill

Read what the rest of the children think about getting to school.

1 What does Greg think about getting to school? Why does he think that?

2 How is Gus's point of view different from Sitta's?

3 What do you think is the best way to get to school? Why do you think that?

Greg	Sitta	Jocelyn
I like to ride my bike to school. My Mom rides with me.	Walking is the best way to get to school. It's nice to be outside.	I ride in the car with my Dad to school. He gets me there on time.

Sharing News and Ideas

► **Vocabulary**
communicate
communication

◎ **Reading Skill**
Sequence

⬭ → ⬭ → ⬭

Build on What You Know

Do you talk on the telephone? Using the telephone is one way to share news.

People Communicate

When people **communicate,** they share news and ideas. Two ways to communicate are talking and writing. The way people share news and ideas is called **communication.**

main ★ idea

These children communicate with sign language.

Communication Inventions

Long, long ago people made cave pictures to communicate their ideas. Later they invented alphabets. <u>Inventions</u> (★ main idea) <u>made communication easier and faster.</u>

People used to write books by hand. An invention called the printing press helped make books more quickly. Then more people had books. They learned to read and shared ideas from the books they read.

A printing press from the past

Review In what ways do you communicate?

Inventions Timeline

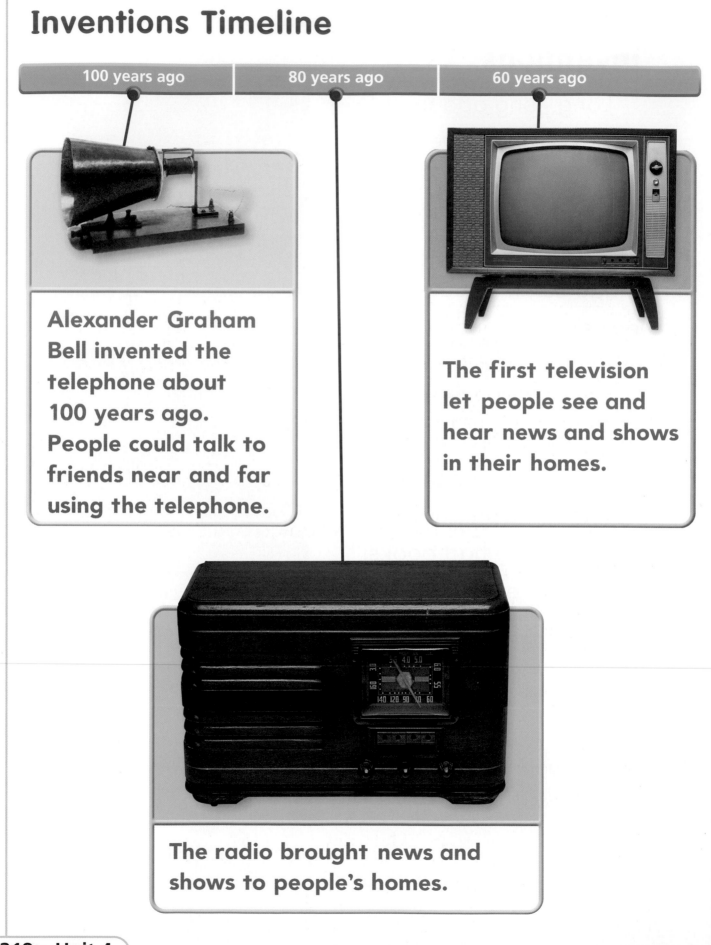

100 years ago

80 years ago

60 years ago

Alexander Graham Bell invented the telephone about 100 years ago. People could talk to friends near and far using the telephone.

The first television let people see and hear news and shows in their homes.

The radio brought news and shows to people's homes.

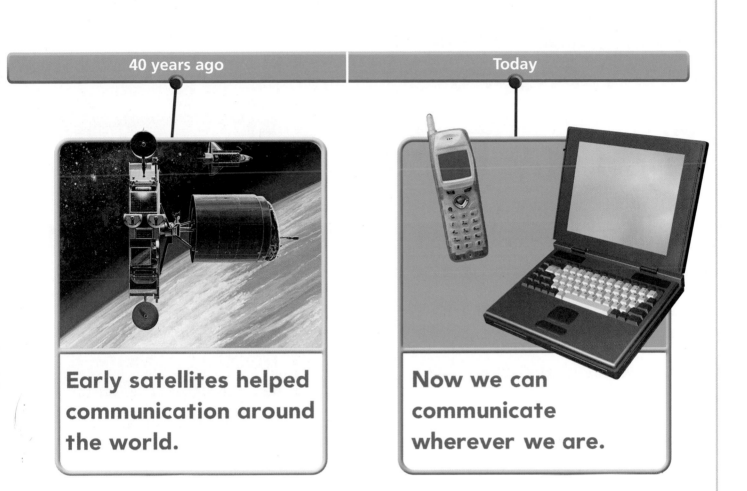

40 years ago	Today

Early satellites helped communication around the world.

Now we can communicate wherever we are.

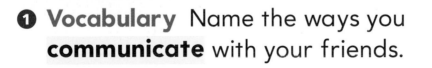

Review Tell ways that communication has changed from the past.

Lesson Review

❶ **Vocabulary** Name the ways you **communicate** with your friends.

❷ **Main Idea** What are two communication inventions?

HANDS ON **Activity** Make a chart of communication inventions that you use.

The Pony Express

Long ago people who lived in the western part of the United States had to wait months for mail to come. In 1860, the Pony Express began!

The Pony Express was a new and fast way to move the mail. Abraham Lincoln had become President. People in the West wanted news about him.

It took just seven days and 19 hours for Abraham Lincoln's first speech to arrive in California. People could not believe how fast the news had come!

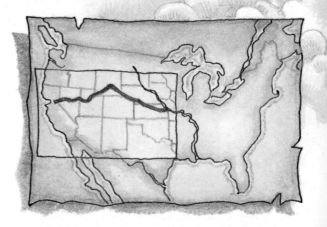

Activities

1. **Talk About It** What are some ways that people can send mail today?

2. **Think About It** Why do you think it is important to get news quickly?

Big Idea

The Big Idea

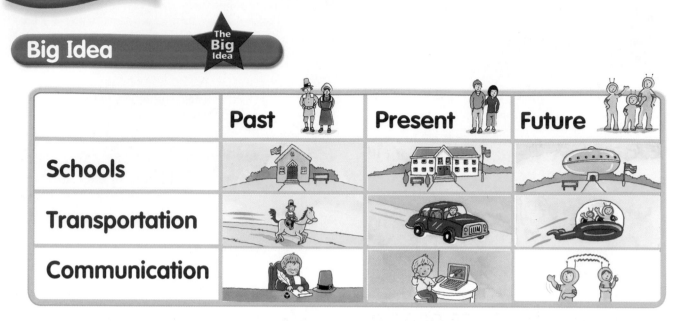

	Past	Present	Future
Schools			
Transportation			
Communication			

Fill in the missing words that help describe the chart.

1. The _____ is time that has not happened yet. (page 178)
2. In the past, people used horses for _____. (page 208)
3. In the present, we use computers and telephones for _____. (page 216)

Facts and Main Ideas

4. Why was life hard for the Pilgrims at first? (page 190)

5. What is different about schools long ago and schools today? (page 202)

6. What kinds of transportation today are faster than transportation long ago? (page 208)

7. What are some communication inventions you use every day? (page 219)

Write the letter for each correct answer.

8. A new way of doing something

9. The time that is now

10. A story about the past

11. All the things people learn

A. **history** (page 177)

B. **present** (page 176)

C. **invention** (page 209)

D. **communication** (page 216)

E. **education** (page 215)

✔ **Test Practice**

12. What does the word **harvest** mean?

   A. An invention in the past

   B. Crops that are gathered

   C. A factory where food is made

   D. A place where settlers live

Critical Thinking

Sequence

13. Who were the first people to live in North America?

14. Who came next?

Review and Test Prep

Use a Timeline

The Pilgrims' Harvest Timeline

1621

Spring   Summer   Fall

15. What did the Pilgrims do first?

16. What happened during the summer?

Compare Points of View

17. Why does Deb think that Thanksgiving is the best holiday?

18. Do you agree with Deb's point of view? Why or why not?

"Thanksgiving is the best holiday. I like to eat good food with my family."

—Deb

Unit Activity

Make an Accordion Book

Think about changes in your life.

❶ Fold a sheet of paper in four parts just like in the picture.

❷ Draw and write about your past, present and future on the four parts.

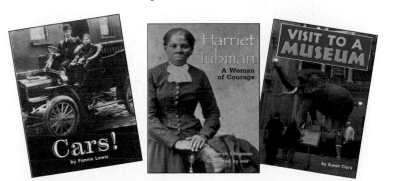

CURRENT EVENTS

WEEKLY (WR) READER

Current Events

Create **History in the News** puppets. Find current events from Weekly Reader on the social studies website.

Technology

Current Events Project
eduplace.com/kids/hmss05/

In Your Classroom

Look for these Social Studies Independent Books in your classroom.

Cars!
by Fannie Lewis

Harriet Tubman A Woman of Courage

VISIT TO A MUSEUM
by Susan Clark

At the Library

Look for these books at your library.

Aunt Claire's Yellow Beehive Hair
by Deborah Blumenthal

William's House
by Ginger Howard

Good Citizens

'Tis the star-spangled
banner, oh, long may
it wave
O'er the land of the
free and the home
of the brave!

—From "The Star-Spangled Banner"
by Francis Scott Key

The
Big
Idea

What do good
citizens do?

Good Citizens

Vocabulary Preview

Technology
e • glossary
e • word games
www.eduplace.com/kids/hmss05/

President

The **President** is the leader of the United States government. Abraham Lincoln is a past President.

page 236

government

A **government** is a group of people who are chosen to run a community, a state, or a country. page 231

Reading Strategy

Question Use the question strategy in Lessons 1, 2, and 3.
Predict and Infer Use the predict and infer strategy in Lessons 4 and 5.

vote

When people **vote,** they make a choice.

page 246

symbol

The flag is a **symbol** of our country. It stands for freedom.

page 258

People Need Laws

Build on What You Know

What class rules do you follow? Did you know that communities have written rules too?

Laws

A community rule is called a **law.** A community needs laws. Laws help keep a community safe, clean, and fair for everyone.

main idea

Signs That Show Laws

STOP	Children cross here.	NO PARKING ANY TIME
All cars must stop.	Children cross here.	Do not park here.

People Help With Laws

A **government** is a group of people chosen to make laws. There are community, state, and country governments. People can work to make and to change laws.

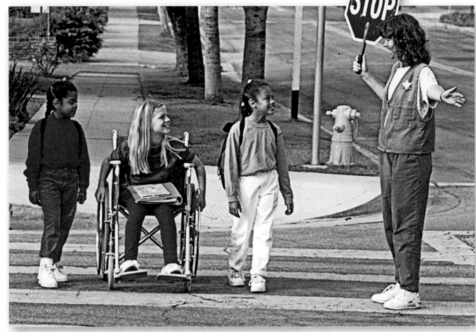

The crossing guard is a community helper.

Review What are ways people help with laws?

Lesson Review

1. **Vocabulary** Tell about one **law** in your community.

2. **Main Idea** Why does a community need laws?

   HANDS ON **Activity** Make a sign that shows a law in your community.

Laws Every Day

Breakfast Time

Food Laws

Many foods must have labels. A label shows what was used to make the food.

Nutrition Facts
Serving Size   1 cup
Servings Per
Container   About 17

Ingredients
Corn Flour
Wheat Flour
Brown Sugar

School Time

Bus Laws

The stop sign on a bus tells cars to stop so children can be safe.

STOP

Play Time

Toy Laws

Labels tell how to use toys safely. They tell how old a child should be to use the toy.

WARNING
not for children
under age 3

Activities

1. **Make It** Think about toys. Make a label that tells how to use a toy safely.

2. **Write About It** Write a sentence about a law that helps keep you safe.

Express Ideas in Writing

► **Vocabulary**
  clearly

Writing **clearly** helps people understand your ideas. You can write clearly about rules.

Learn the Skill

These are the steps Julia followed when she wrote about a classroom rule.

I wait for my turn on the swings.
Julia S.

Step 1 First Julia thought of a rule. Wait for your turn.

Step 2 Julia drew a picture of herself following the rule. Where is Julia in her picture?

Step 3 Then Julia wrote a complete sentence about her rule.

Practice the Skill

Now write your own ideas about classroom rules. Use the pictures and the directions.

1 Think of a rule in your school.

2 Draw a picture of yourself following the rule.

3 Write a sentence about the rule.

A sentence tells a complete idea.

A sentence tells **who** does something.

A sentence tells **what** the person does.

I raise my hand when I want to talk.
Jason W.

Government and Leaders

▶ **Vocabulary**

mayor

governor

President

Reading Skill

**Main idea and
Details**

Build on What You Know

Your teacher is a leader.
Governments have leaders too.

Government

There are governments of
cities and towns, of states, and
of the country. Each place has a
main government building.

main idea (★)

Your community may have a
city or town hall. There may be
a capitol building in your state.

In Washington, D.C., there is
the White House and other
government buildings.

City or town hall

State capitol building

White House

Review What are names of buildings where government leaders work?

Government Leaders

In the United States, government leaders are chosen by the people. Each leader works to make our country a good place to live.

main idea (★)

Mayor

A **mayor** is the leader of a city or town government. A community government takes care of many things such as schools and libraries.

City Mayor

Governor

A **governor** is the leader of a state government. State governments take care of state roads, colleges, and parks.

State Governor

The President

The **President** is the leader of the United States government. The President helps to make laws for all people living in the United States. He also works with leaders around the world.

President

President of the United States

Review Who is the President of the United States?

Past Presidents

There have been government leaders from the time our country was new. Read about three past Presidents.

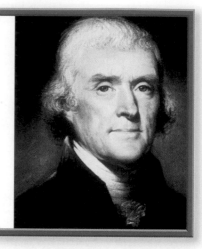

Thomas Jefferson

Thomas Jefferson was the third President. Before he was President, Thomas Jefferson wrote the Declaration of Independence.

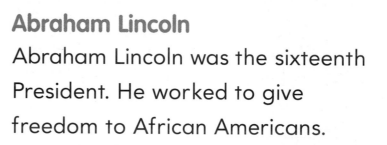

Abraham Lincoln

Abraham Lincoln was the sixteenth President. He worked to give freedom to African Americans.

Franklin Delano Roosevelt

When Franklin Delano Roosevelt became President, many people were out of work. He helped to pass laws that gave people jobs.

Leaders Long Ago

There have been government leaders for thousands of years. Here are three leaders from the past. We still remember them today.

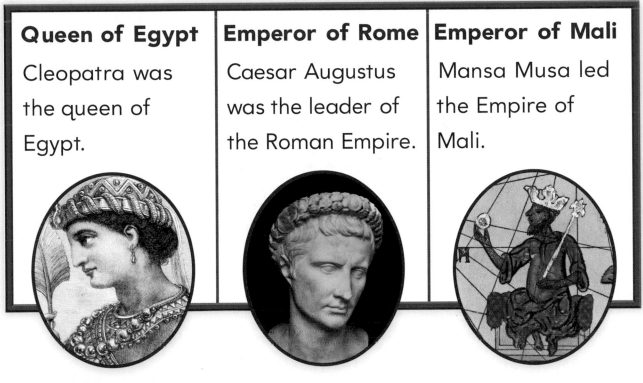

Queen of Egypt	Emperor of Rome	Emperor of Mali
Cleopatra was the queen of Egypt.	Caesar Augustus was the leader of the Roman Empire.	Mansa Musa led the Empire of Mali.

Review Why do governments need leaders?

Lesson Review

❶ **Vocabulary** Tell something you know about a **governor.**

❷ **Main Idea** What is different about the work of a mayor, a governor, and the President?

Activity Draw and tell about a government leader long ago or today.

George Washington

George Washington was the first President of the United States. He is known as the Father of His Country because he was the first leader of our new country.

President George Washington made a promise to follow the Constitution. The Constitution is a plan for making laws for the United States. Every new President makes the same promise.

The Constitution of the United States of America.

Activities

1. Talk About It Tell about the patriotism of George Washington.

2. Make It Make a fact card about George Washington.

Technology Read more biographies. www.eduplace.com/kids/hmss05/

Citizens

Vocabulary

right

responsibility

vote

election

Reading Skill

Main Idea and Details

Build on What You Know

Why is it important to be a good helper in your community and in our country?

Citizens Have Rights

Citizens of the United States have rights. A **right** is something you are free to do.

main
(★)
idea

RIGHTS

☆ Right to choose leaders

☆ Right to privacy

☆ Right to be a part of a group

Betsy and Dan Nally collect turkeys and give them to families who have no money to buy Thanksgiving dinner.

Citizens Have Responsibilities

Citizens have responsibilities. A **responsibility** is a duty to do something. One responsibility citizens have is to help to make laws and to follow them. Good citizens can help to make their country a better place to live.

main idea (★)

Review What are some ways that you can be a good citizen?

Citizens Make Choices

Sometimes people in a group want to do different things. People can vote to decide which thing to do. When people **vote**, they make a choice. Voting is a fair way for groups to make decisions.

(★) main idea

Tim votes to go to the aquarium. He will put his ballot in the box.

Ballot

Where will we go for our field trip?

☒ Aquarium

☐ Dairy farm

Ballot Box

Citizens choose their government leaders in an election. An **election** is a time when citizens vote for the leader they think will do the best job. The winner is the one with the most votes. Citizens can vote for rules and laws too. Voting is a responsibility.

Review What things have you voted on in school?

Lesson Review

1. **Vocabulary** What do citizens **vote** for in an election?

2. **Main Idea** What responsibilities does a citizen have?

➤ **Activity** Write about a field trip you would vote for. Why is that a good choice?

From VOTE!

★ ★ ★ ★ ★ ★ ★ ★

by Eileen Christelow

In this book, Chris Smith wants to be the mayor of her city.

Voting is a way to choose.

Those people want to vote for Bill Brown.

Vote? What's that?

Activities

1. **Talk About It** Tell why it is important to vote.

2. **Try It** Vote for a favorite class book. Add up the class votes to find out which book your class likes best. Then give an oral report.

Heroes in Our Country

Build on What You Know

Think of someone in your community who helps other people.

What Makes A Hero?

A **hero** does something brave or works hard to help others. Heroes can be strong, kind, honest, or caring. Heroes don't give up when things are hard.

main idea (★)

Sacagawea

American Indian Guide
Sacagawea helped two American explorers named Lewis and Clark. She was a Shoshone who helped Lewis and Clark talk to American Indians.

Harriet Tubman

Leader for Freedom

Harriet Tubman led many African Americans to freedom. Long ago, African Americans in our country were not free to choose their work or their homes.

Susan B. Anthony

Leader for Women's Rights

Susan B. Anthony worked to get women the right to vote. Before 1920, women could not vote for leaders or laws.

Review How did these heroes help others?

Eleanor Roosevelt

World Leader for Rights

Eleanor Roosevelt believed that all people should have the same rights. She worked in our country and around the world.

Cesar Chavez

Leader for Farm Workers

Cesar Chavez worked to get farm workers better pay and safer workplaces.

Dr. Martin Luther King, Jr.

Leader for Equal Rights

Dr. King was a church leader. He worked to get equal rights for African Americans. He led marches and gave famous speeches to help change unfair laws.

Review Why do we remember these heroes?

Lesson Review

❶ **Vocabulary** Tell about a **hero** you have learned about.

❷ **Main Idea** What makes someone a hero?

HANDS ON **Activity** Write two sentences about a person that you think is a hero. Draw a picture of that person.

Hero Dogs

What is furry with four legs and is a hero? A guide dog is a hero every day.

Young dogs go to school to learn how to be guide dogs for the blind.

The dog helps the owner cross a busy street.

Guide dogs are heroes for the work they do. So are their owners who put their lives in the care of these dogs.

Activities

1. **Talk About It** Why do you think guide dogs are heroes?

2. **Write It** Make a list of other dog heroes such as police dogs.

Compare Fact and Fiction

▶ **Vocabulary**
fiction
nonfiction
fact

Made-up stories are **fiction. Nonfiction** books tell facts. A **fact** is something true.

Learn the Skill

Step 1 Read the title of this book. It is a biography. Biographies are books about real people.

Step 2 Look at the words and pictures. The words tell facts about Mae Jemison. The pictures show real women.

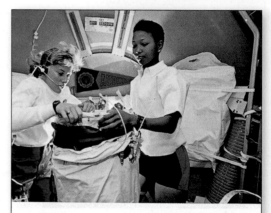

Finally, on September 12, 1992, Mae's dream of flying into space came true. For eight days, the crew of the *Endeavour* circled the Earth. Mae ran scientific and medical experiments about bones, weightlessness, and motion sickness. All her years of study had finally paid off.

15

Step 3 Decide if this book is fiction or nonfiction. What makes you think so?

Practice the Skill

Look at the two books. Then follow the directions.

1 Choose the book that you think is fiction. Tell why you think it is fiction.

2 Choose the book you think tells facts. Explain why you think that book has facts.

Symbols of Our Country

Vocabulary

symbol

honor

Reading Skill

Classify

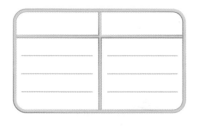

Build on What You Know

Do you say the "Pledge of Allegiance" to the flag each day?

Stars and Stripes

Our flag is a symbol for our country. A **symbol** is a picture, place, or thing that stands for something else.

main idea

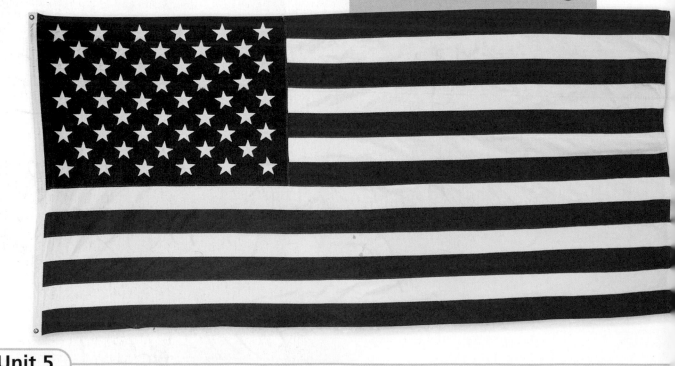

The American Flag

The flag has red and white stripes. It has 50 stars, one for each state.

Uncle Sam is also a symbol. The first letters of Uncle Sam are the same as in the United States.

Review Why do you think Uncle Sam is dressed as he is?

This boy is dressed as Uncle Sam.

Symbols of Freedom

We **honor** symbols of the (★) main idea United States to show that our country is important to us. The Liberty Bell and the bald eagle are symbols of freedom.

The Liberty Bell

The bald eagle stands for a strong country.

The Statue of Liberty is a symbol of welcome for our country.

Review What symbols have you seen?

Places As Symbols

Places can be symbols <u>main idea</u> ★ too. Look at the map of Washington, D.C. Find buildings that are symbols. The Lincoln Memorial honors President Abraham Lincoln. The Washington Monument honors President George Washington.

The White House is in Washington, D.C.

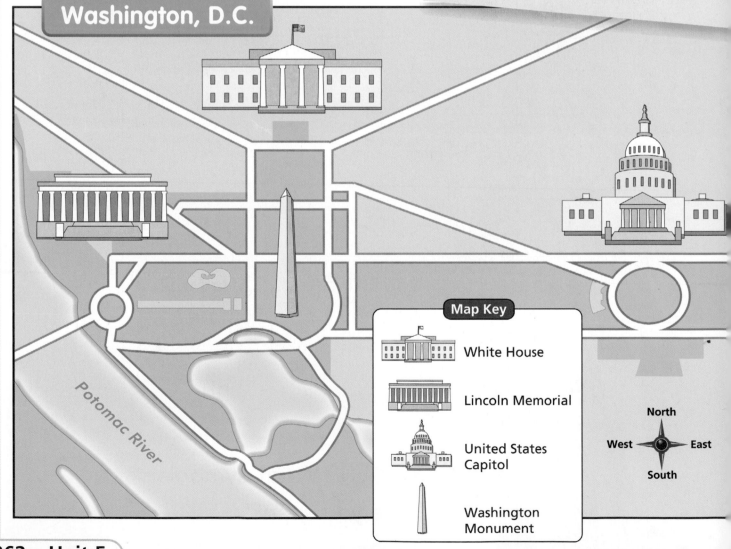

Washington, D.C.

Potomac River

Map Key

White House

Lincoln Memorial

United States Capitol

Washington Monument

North
West — East
South

The Lincoln Memorial is also in Washington, D.C.

Mount Rushmore shows the faces of four past Presidents.

Review Name a place that is a symbol for our country.

Lesson Review

❶ **Vocabulary** Tell why we **honor** symbols of our country.

❷ **Main Idea** Why does our country have symbols?

Activity Write about three symbols you like.

Make a Post Card

Pretend you visited the places shown on pages 262 and 263. Choose your favorite symbol. Make a post card of that symbol.

Step 1: Draw a picture of a symbol on the card.

Step 2: Write your post card to a friend. Write about the symbol.

Step 3: Write your friend's address.

Hi Betty,
The Statue of
Liberty wears a
crown and carries
a torch.
       Your friend,
       Ava

Betty Zimmer
Mrs. Santiago's Class
Stone Elementary School
City, State 00000

Big Idea

Responsible Citizens

A.   B.

Match the words to the correct picture above.

1. follow laws (page 231)

2. vote (page 246)

Facts and Main Ideas

3. Why do we honor symbols of our country? (page 258)

4. How do people choose a President or a governor? (page 247)

5. Why are some people called heroes? (page 250)

6. Why do we have elections? (page 236)

Write the letter or word for each correct answer.

7. A community rule is called a _____ .

8. The flag is a _____ of our country.

9. The group of people chosen to run a country is called the _____ .

10. The _____ is the leader of our country.

> **A. governor** (page 238)
>
> **B. law** (page 230)
>
> **C. symbol** (page 258)
>
> **D. President** (page 236)
>
> **E. government** (page 231)

✔ Test Practice

11. The word **election** means _____ .

    A. the leader of a state

    B. someone who is a hero

    C. a time when people vote

    D. a symbol of our country

Critical Thinking

Summarize

12. Why do governments need leaders?

Skillbuilders

Compare Fact and Fiction

Ben Franklin invented bifocal glasses.

1

Ben could not read without his glasses.

2

13. Which numbered page is fiction?

14. Which page tells true facts?

Express Ideas in Writing

Think of someone who is a good leader from your home, school, or country. Then answer the question below.

15. Why do you think that person is a good leader? Give at least two reasons why you think so.

Unit Activity

The Big Idea

Make a Hero Poster

Think of a hero in your community.

❶ Write the words **My Hero** on the top of a paper.

❷ Write your hero's name. Draw pictures and write words to show what your hero has done.

CURRENT EVENTS
WEEKLY (WR) READER

Current Events Project

Make biography cards for **Heroes in the News.** Find current events from Weekly Reader on the social studies website.

Technology

Current Events Project
www.eduplace.com/kids/hmss05/

In Your Classroom

Look for these Social Studies Independent Books in your classroom.

At the Library

Look for these books at your library.

America is . . .
by Louise Borden

Martin's Big Words: The Life of Dr. Martin Luther King, Jr.
by Doreen Rappaport

Holiday Lessons

Columbus Day

Columbus Day is named for the explorer Christopher Columbus.

In 1492, Columbus and his men sailed in three ships from Spain to North America. On Columbus Day people remember how the voyage of Columbus changed the world.

Activity

Walnut Shell Ship

1. Use paper and a toothpick to make a sail.

2. Stick some clay into a walnut shell. Stick the sail into the clay.

3. Sail your ship around the globe. Do you know which way Columbus went?

271

Veterans Day

Veterans Day is a day to honor people who have fought in wars.

Many veterans wear uniforms and march in parades on Veterans Day. People thank our veterans for helping to keep our country safe.

Activity

Thank You Posters

1. Make a poster to honor veterans. You may want to draw a picture on your poster.

2. Write why we honor veterans on your poster.

In honor of the brave veterans who fought for their country

Thanksgiving Day

On Thanksgiving Day, people give thanks for all they have. A time for Thanksgiving began with the Pilgrims. They shared a feast with the Wampanoag.

Today many families celebrate Thanksgiving Day by eating turkey dinners. Familes share why they are thankful.

Activity
Thankful Turkeys

1. Trace your hand onto colored paper. Cut out the shape.

2. Write things you are thankful for on each finger.

3. Color the turkey's head.

my family
food to eat
ice cream
sunny days

Martin Luther King, Jr. Day

Dr. Martin Luther King, Jr., was a great leader. He believed in peace and fairness for all people.

Dr. Martin Luther King, Jr., thought that some laws were unfair to African Americans. He worked hard to change the unfair laws. He was given a special Peace Prize for his work.

Activity

Make a Peace Prize

1. Think of someone you know who helps other people.

2. Make a peace prize for that person.

Presidents' Day

On Presidents' Day we honor two great Presidents of the United States, George Washington and Abraham Lincoln.

George Washington was the first President of the United States.

We remember Abraham Lincoln for keeping our country together.

Activity

Make a Bookmark

1. Place a penny or a quarter face side up. Put tissue paper over the coin and rub it with a colored pencil.

2. Glue your picture to a strip of colored paper. Write the President's name.

George Washington

Memorial Day

On Memorial Day, we remember the people who fought and died in United States wars.

On Memorial Day people put flowers and flags on statues and graves. Towns and cities have parades. Citizens honor the people who fought for our country.

Activity

Memorial Day Wreath

1. Cut stars or flower shapes out of colored paper. Glue them around a paper plate.

2. Write a message in the center of your wreath.

For all the soldiers on Memorial Day

Flag Day

On Flag Day, people honor the United States flag. Some communities have parades and sing songs.

The flag stands for our country. The fifty stars on the flag stand for the fifty states.

Activity

Stars and Stripes Pinwheel

1. Color a piece of paper with stars and stripes. What colors will you use?

2. Fold each corner into the middle. Tape the corners down. Attach your pinwheel to a pencil.

Independence Day

On July 4 we celebrate our country's birthday. Our country was born on July 4, 1776. People celebrate Independence Day with parades and picnics. Many communities have fireworks at night.

Activity

United States Birthday Card

1. Fold a piece of paper in half.

2. Write a birthday message for the United States.

References

Citizenship Handbook

Resources

Our Flag

How do you feel when you see the American flag flying from a flag pole? Have you ever tapped your feet to a song about our country? Our country's flag and songs are ways we show we care about the United States.

When we respect the flag, we show pride in the United States. There are rules about how to care for the flag.

The flag must never touch the ground. The flag should be lit at night.

Our Motto

Each country can have its own motto, or saying. A motto reminds people of things that are important to their country. Our country's motto is *e pluribus unum*. This means that Americans can be very different from each other, but we all belong to the same country.

Some coins celebrate people or events. The back of this nickel celebrates the Louisiana Purchase.

Songs of Our Nation

There are many songs people sing to show they love our country. The "Star-Spangled Banner" is our country's song, or anthem. "America" and "God Bless America" are songs that tell why we love our country.

"The Star-Spangled Banner"

by Francis Scott Key

Oh say can you see, by the dawn's early light,

What so proudly we hailed at the twilight's last gleaming?

Whose broad stripes and bright stars, through the
    perilous fight

O'er the ramparts we watched were so gallantly streaming?

And the rockets' red glare, the bomb bursting in air,

Gave proof through the night that our flag was still there.

O say, does that star-spangled banner yet wave

O'er the land of the free and the home of the brave?

"America"
by Samuel F. Smith

My country 'tis of thee
Sweet land of liberty,
　Of thee I sing;
Land where my fathers died
Land of the Pilgrims' pride,
From every mountain side
　Let freedom ring.

"God Bless America"
by Irving Berlin

God bless America,
Land that I love,
Stand beside her and guide her
Through the night with a light from above.
From the mountains, to the prairies,
To the oceans white with foam,
God bless America,
My home sweet home.

When you hear songs about our country, what do you think about?

Character Traits

A character trait is what you see when a person acts. A person who acts bravely shows courage. Courage is a character trait. Some character traits can help you do your best now and when you get older.

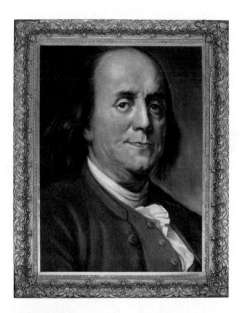

Benjamin Franklin

Civic Virtue Benjamin Franklin worked hard to make the new United States a place where people were free to live and work and speak freely.

Barbara Jordan

Fairness Barbara Jordan was a lawmaker. She worked to pass fair laws for all the people in our country.

Courage means acting bravely. It takes courage to be honest. It takes courage to tell the truth.

Patriotism is being proud of your country. It means working to make the country a good place to live.

Responsibility means doing all your work. You can count on people who show responsibility. They will do all the things they are asked to do.

Respect means listening to what other people want and believe. Showing respect for others helps everyone get along.

Fairness means acting to make things fair for everyone.

Civic virtue means doing things to help people in communities live and work well together.

Caring is helping others. Listening to how other people feel is also caring.

Geographic Terms

forest
a large area of land where many trees grow

▲ **desert**
a dry area where few plants grow

hill
a raised mass of land, smaller than a mountain

▲ **island**
land with water all around it

lake
a body of water with land all around it

mountains

hill

river

lake

ocean

mountain
a steep mass of land, much higher than the surrounding country

▲ **ocean**
a salty body of water covering a large area of the earth

peninsula
land that sticks out into water

plain
a broad, flat area of land

plateau
an area of flat land that is higher than the land around it

river
a large stream of water that runs into a lake, ocean, or another river

valley
low land between mountains or hills

valley

peninsula

plain

Atlas

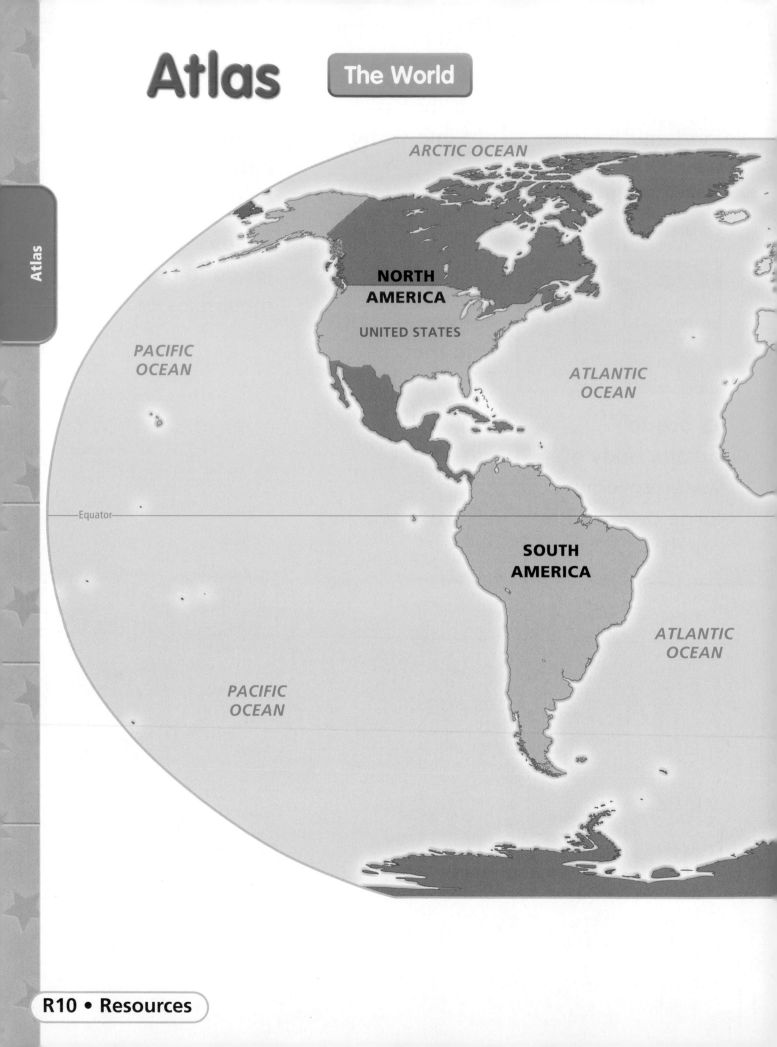

Atlas

ARCTIC OCEAN

NORTH AMERICA

UNITED STATES

PACIFIC OCEAN

ATLANTIC OCEAN

Equator

SOUTH AMERICA

ATLANTIC OCEAN

PACIFIC OCEAN

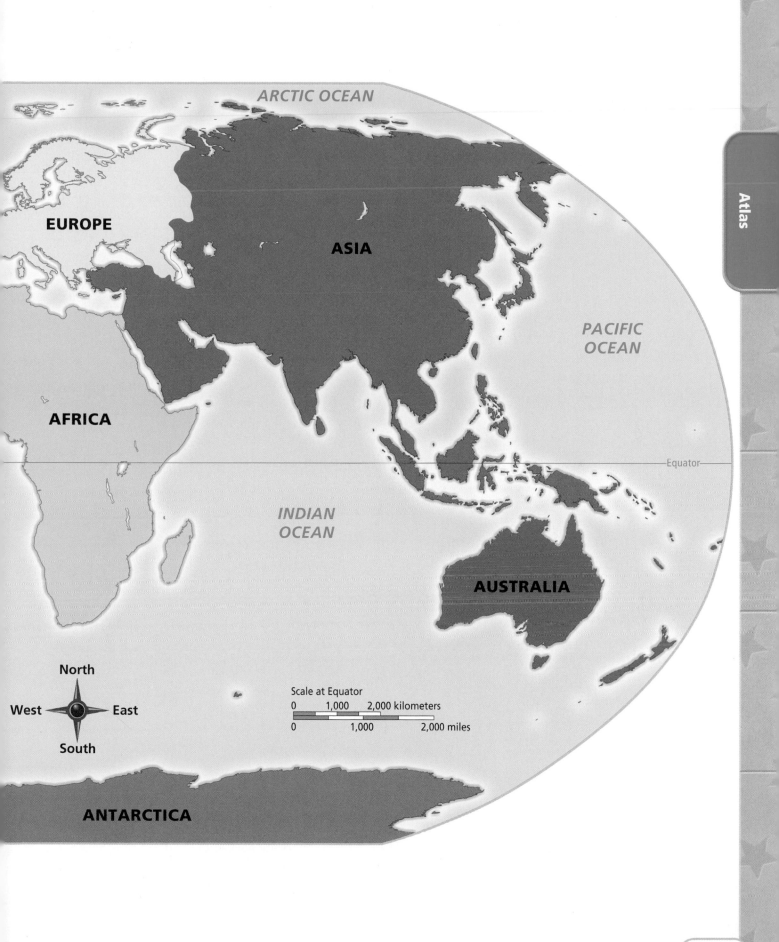

ARCTIC OCEAN

EUROPE

ASIA

PACIFIC
OCEAN

AFRICA

Equator

INDIAN
OCEAN

AUSTRALIA

North

West   East

South

Scale at Equator

0   1,000   2,000 kilometers

0   1,000   2,000 miles

ANTARCTICA

Canada, United States, Mexico

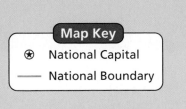

PACIFIC OCEAN

Atlas

ARCTIC OCEAN

CANADA

Ottawa
⊛

UNITED STATES

Washington, D.C.
⊛

ATLANTIC OCEAN

MEXICO

Mexico City
⊛

The United States

ALASKA

0   500 kilometers
0   500 miles

Atlas

WASHINGTON

OREGON

IDAHO

MONTANA

WYOMING

NEVADA

UTAH

COLORADO

CALIFORNIA

ARIZONA

NEW MEXICO

North
West   East
South

Map Key

⊛   National Capital

—   National Boundary

—   State Boundary

HAWAII

0   200 kilometers
0   200 miles

NEW
HAMPSHIRE

VERMONT

MAINE

MASSACHUSETTS

NORTH
DAKOTA

MINNESOTA

NEW
YORK

RHODE
ISLAND

SOUTH
DAKOTA

WISCONSIN

MICHIGAN

CONNECTICUT

IOWA

PENNSYLVANIA

NEW
JERSEY

NEBRASKA

OHIO

DELAWARE

INDIANA

WEST
VIRGINIA

Washington, D.C.

ILLINOIS

MARYLAND

VIRGINIA

KANSAS

MISSOURI

KENTUCKY

NORTH
CAROLINA

TENNESSEE

OKLAHOMA

ARKANSAS

SOUTH
CAROLINA

ALABAMA

GEORGIA

MISSISSIPPI

TEXAS

LOUISIANA

FLORIDA

0   125   250 kilometers

0   125   250 miles

Picture Glossary

American Indians

American Indians were the first people to live in North America. (page 184)
The Cherokee is one group of **American Indians.**

buyer

A buyer is a person who pays money for goods or service. (page 160)
This **buyer** pays for food.

calendar

A calendar is a chart that shows days, weeks, months, and years. (page 34)
People use a **calendar** to help them remember special days.

citizen

A citizen is a person who belongs to a place. (page 111)
You are a **citizen** of the country where you live.

city

A city is a place where many people live close to one another. (page 102)
A **city** can have many tall buildings.

communication

The way people share news and ideas. (page 216)
Sign language is one kind of **communication.**

community

A community is a place where people live and work together. (page 54)
A town is a **community** that has homes, stores, and schools.

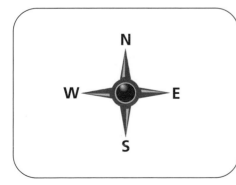

compass rose

A compass rose is a symbol that shows the direction for north, south, east, and west. (page 166)
A **compass rose** helps people find places on a map.

continent

A continent is a very large area of land. (page 76)
North America is the **continent** where we live.

cost

The cost is the amount of money that is needed to buy something. (page 144)
How much does the pencil **cost**?

country

A country is land where people live under one government. (page 60)
The United States is the **country** where you live.

D

distance

Distance is the amount of space between two points. (page 108)
It is a short **distance** between the home and the bakery.

E

education

Things people learn, such as math, history, and reading is called education. (page 205)
Children go to school to get an **education.**

election

An election is a time when citizens vote. (page 247)
In an **election,** people can vote for government leaders.

F

fact

A fact is something that is true. (page 256)
It is a **fact** that Abraham Lincoln was a past President.

factory

A factory is a place where workers use machines to make goods. (page 154)
Orange juice is made in a **factory.**

family

A family is a group of people who care about each other. (page 26)
This **family** shares a meal.

fiction

Fiction is a type of story that is not real. (page 256)
Dog's Party is a **fiction** book.

future

The future is time after today. (page 178)
Tomorrow, next week, and next year are all time in the **future.**

⭐G

globe

A globe is a model of Earth. (page 80)
The **globe** shows Earth's continents and oceans.

goods

Goods are things we buy or use. (page 139)
A bakery sells **goods** such as rolls and breads.

government

Government is the group of people who run a community, state, or country. (page 231)
People who work in **government** make laws.

governor

A governor is the leader of state government. (page 238)
Who is the **governor** of your state?

⭐ H

harvest

A harvest is the crops that are ready to be gathered. (page 195)
The Pilgrims were thankful for a good **harvest.**

hero

A hero is a person who does something brave or who works hard to help others. (page 250)
Martin Luther King, Jr. was a **hero.**

history

History is the story of what happened in the past. (page 177)
We learn about people who lived long ago when we read **history.**

honor

Honor means to show that someone or something is important to us. (page 260)
We **honor** our country when we say the "Pledge of Allegiance."

invention

An invention is a new tool or way of doing something. (page 209)
The car was a great **invention.**

job

A job is work that must get done. (page 37)
Hanging up my coat is a **job.**

L

lake

A lake is a body of water that has land all around it. (page 85)
A **lake** can be a good place to swim or ride a boat.

law

A law is a community rule. (page 230)
It is a **law** that cars must stop at a stop sign.

leader

A leader is a person who is in charge of a group of people. (page 44)
A principal is the **leader** of a school.

M

machine

A machine is an object that does work for people. (page 160)
A **machine** can sort raisins.

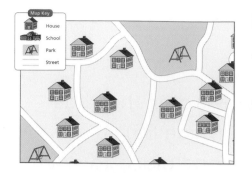

map

A map is a drawing of a place that shows a view from above. (page 42)
The **map** shows where the park is.

map key

The map key is the set of symbols found on a map. (page 52)
This **map key** shows the symbol for river.

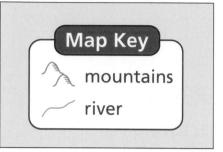

mayor

The mayor is the leader of a city or town government. (page 238)
The **mayor** visited our school.

mountain

A mountain is land that is higher than all the land around it. (page 82)
Mt. McKinley is the highest **mountain** in our country.

natural resource

A natural resource is something in nature that people use. (page 88) Water is a very important **natural resource** for our lives.

needs

Needs are the things people must have to live. (page 130) Homes are **needs** for all people.

neighbors

People who live near each other are called neighbors. (page 116) Jamal has many nice **neighbors.**

ocean

Pacific Ocean

An ocean is a large body of salty water. (page 75) The Pacific **Ocean** is the world's largest ocean.

past

The past is the time that happened before today. (page 176)

In the **past,** you were a baby.

picture graph

A graph that uses pictures to show numbers of things is a picture graph. (page 150)

A **picture graph** can show who has the most people in their family.

plain

A plain is a large, flat land area. (page 83)

A **plain** can be grassy.

present

The present is the time that is happening today. (page 176)

In the **present,** you are in first grade.

President

The President is the leader of the United States government. (page 239)
George Washington was the first **President** of our country.

responsibility

A responsibility is a duty to do something. (page 245)
One **responsibility** a citizen has is to obey laws.

right

Something you are free to do is called a right. (page 244)
Citizens of our country have the **right** to speak freely.

river

A river is a body of fresh water that moves across the land. (page 84)
The Missouri **River** is the longest river in our country.

rule

A rule is a statement or an idea that tells people what they must do. (page 43)
Sit on the slide is a playground **rule.**

⭐ **S**

save

To save means to put away and keep. (page 147)
Many people **save** money in a bank.

season

A season is a time of year with its own weather. (page 97)
Winter is usually the coldest **season.**

sell

To sell means to trade goods or services for money. (page 138)
Farmers can **sell** the food they grow to people who live in cities.

seller

A seller is a person who has goods or services that others can buy. (page 160)
This **seller** has many pets for sale.

Picture Glossary

services

Jobs people do to help others are called services. (page 139)
A doctor gives many health **services.**

settlers

People who come to live in a new place are called settlers. (page 191)
The Pilgrims were **settlers** in a new land.

Ohio

state

A state is a larger community made up of cities, suburbs, and towns. (page 110)
Ohio is a **state** in our country.

suburb

A suburb is a town that is close to a city. (page 103)
Many people who live in a **suburb** work in the city.

symbol

A symbol is a picture, place, or thing that stands for something else. (page 258)
Uncle Sam is a **symbol** of our country.

timeline

A timeline shows when events happened. (page 182)
A **timeline** can show the big events in your life.

town

A community that is smaller than a city is called a town. (page 103)
A **town** has fewer homes and schools than a city.

transportation

Ways to move people and things from place to place is called transportation. (page 208)
A train is one kind of **transportation.**

volunteers

Volunteers are people who choose to work for no money. (page 139)
Joan and Charles are **volunteers** who help paint houses.

vote

When you vote, you make a choice. (page 246)

When citizens are 18 years old, they can **vote** for government leaders.

wants

Wants are things people would like to have. (page 132)

Having many, many toys are **wants** a child might have.

weather

Weather is what the air outside is like. (page 96)

Clouds are part of **weather.**

worker

A person who does a job is called a worker. (page 152)

A factory **worker** makes goods.

Index

Page numbers with *m* after them refer to maps. Page numbers in italics refer to pictures.

Index

Index

Index

Index

Index

Acknowledgments

Acknowledgments

Excerpt from "A Family is a Family," by Skip West. Copyright © Skip West. Reprinted by permission of Skip West, ewest@stny.rr.com.

"God Bless America," by Irving Berlin. © Copyright 1938, 1939, © copyright renewed 1965, 1966 by Irving Berlin. © Copyright assigned to the Trustees of the God Bless America Fund. International Copyright Secured. All Rights Reserved. Reprinted by permission of the Irving Berlin Music Company.

Excerpt from Jingle Dancer, by Cynthia Leitich Smith, illustrated by Cornelius Van Wright and Ying-Hwa Hu. Text copyright © 2000 by Cynthia Leitich Smith. Illustrations copyright © 2000 by Cornelius Van Wright and Ying-Hwa Hu. Reprinted by permission of HarperCollins Publishers and Curtis Brown Ltd.

"Moon of Falling Leaves," from Thirteen Moons on Turtle's Back, by Joseph Bruchac and Jonathan London. Text copyright © 1992 by Joseph Bruchac and Jonathan London. Used by permission of Philomel Books, a division of Penguin Young Readers Group, a member of Penguin Group (USA) Inc., 345 Hudson Street, New York, NY 10014. All rights reserved.

"Our Planet Earth," from Sing of the Earth and Sky, by Aileen Fisher. Copyright © 2001 by Aileen Fisher. Reprinted by permission of Boyds Mills Press, Inc., A Highlights Company.

Excerpt from Rush Hour, by Christine Loomis. Text copyright © 1996 by Christine Loomis. Reprinted by permission of Houghton Mifflin Company.

Excerpt from The Saturday Escape, by Daniel J. Mahoney. Copyright © 2000 by Daniel J. Mahoney. Reprinted by permission of Houghton Mifflin Company.

Excerpt from "Spell Song," by Kwakiutl, from Weave Little Stars Into My Sleep, edited by Neil Philip. Compilation, reworkings, and afterword copyright © 2001 by Neil Philip. Reprinted by permission of Houghton Mifflin Company.

Excerpt from Tattered Sails, by Verla Kay, illustrated by Dan Andreasen. Text copyright © 2001 by Verla Kay Bradley. Illustrations copyright © 2001 by Dan Andreasen. Used by permission of G. P. Putnam's Sons, a division of Penguin Young Readers Group, a member of Penguin Group (USA) Inc., 345 Hudson Street, New York, NY 10014 and Curtis Brown, Ltd. All rights reserved.

Excerpt from Vote!, by Eileen Christelow. Copyright © 2003 by Eileen Christelow. Reprinted by permission of Houghton Mifflin Company.

Excerpt from "You Always Have to Pay," from City Poems, by Lois Lenski. Text copyright © 1954, 1956, 1965, 1971 by Lois Lenski. Reprinted by permission of Steven Covey, son of Lois Lenski.

Photography Credits

22–23 Ariel Skelley/Corbis. 24 (cl) Rob & Sas/Corbis. 24–25 (b) Jim Cummins/Taxi/Getty Images. 25 (tl) Stone/Getty Images. 26 Tom & Dee Ann McCarthy/Corbis. 27 (b) Tom & Dee Ann McCarthy/Corbis; (t) Jim Cummins/Getty Images. 28 (l) Michael Keller/Corbis; (r) Masterfile. 29 Jose Luis Pelaez, Inc./Corbis. 36 Tom Prettyman/Photo Edit Inc. 37 (br) David Young–Wolfe/Photo Edit; (lc) Michael Newman/Photo Edit. 38 Bruce Burkhardt/Corbis. 42 Spencer Grant/Photo Edit. 44 Image Source Limited/Index Stock Imagery. 45 Richard Hutchings/Photo Edit. 46–47 'Int Int'l/Estock Photo/PictureQuest. 55 (l) Rosemary Cloud City of East Point Fire Department; (r) Courtesy of Catherine Beyers. 56 (bl) Jeff Dunn/Index Stock Imagery; (tl) Chuck Savage/Corbis; (tr) Hirb Collection/Index Stock Imagery. 57 Ronnie Kaufman/Corbis. 58 (c) Rosemary Cloud City of East Point Fire Department. 58–59 (b) SuperStock/ PictureQuest. 60 Bettmann/Corbis. 61 Courtesy of Katia Lemos. 62 (bl) Jacob Halaska/Index Stock Photography; (br) Corbis. 63 Catherine Karnow/Corbis. 64 Rick Egan. 65 (bkgd) Paul A. Souders/ Corbis; (inset) Dynamic Graphics, Inc/Creatas. 66 Rubberball Productions/Getty Images. 70–71 B.S.P.I./Corbis. 72 (r) Jim Steinberg/Photo Researchers. 73 (l) ML Sinibaldi/Corbis; 73 (r) Phoebe Dunn/Stock Connection/PictureQuest. 77 (l) Adalberto Rios Szalav /Sexto Sol/Photodisc/Getty Images; (r) Photo 24/Brand X/Getty Images. 82–83 (bkgd) Frank Staub/Index Stock Imagery/PictureQuest. 83 (c) MacDuff Everton/Corbis. 84 (bkgd) Joseph Sohm; Chromosohm Inc./Corbis; (inset) CC Lockwood/Bruce Coleman. 86 (tl) Corbis. 86–87 (bkgd) Michael McQueen/Photographer's Choice/Getty Images. 88 Corbis. 89 (bl) Tom Algire/ Superstock; (br) W. Cody/Corbis. 89 (t) J. A. Kraulis/ Masterfile. 90 (b) Arthur Tilley/i2i Images/PictureQuest; (tr) Peter Christopher/Masterfile. 91 Craig Hammell/Corbis. 92 (br) F. Damm/Masterfile; (cl) ©HMCo./Photodisc.(t) Siede Preis/Photodisc/Getty Images. 92–93 (bkgd) R. Gerth/Masterfile. 93 (b) ©HMCo./C Squared Studios/ Photodisc; (c) ©HMCo./Photodisc; (t) ©HMCo./Photodisc. 97 (bl) Peter Christopher/Masterfile; (br) Bill Bachmann/ Photo Edit. (tl) Dennis Lane/Index Stock Imagery; (tr) Richard Hutchings/Photo Edit. 98 (br) Greg Scott/Masterfile; (tr) Rommel/Masterfile. 99 (cl) Rommel/Masterfile; (tr) Rubberball. 101 ©HMCo./Morocco Flowers. 102 Joseph Sohm/Corbis. 103 Dennis O'Clair/Stone/Getty Images. 106–107 (bkgd) Jeff Greenburg/Photo Edit. 107 (inset) Corbis. 112 (t) Galen Rowell/Corbis. 112–113 (bkgd) Rick Bostick/Index Stock Imagery. 113 (tl) James Shaffer/Photo Edit; (tr) Bill Ross/Corbis. 116 ©HMCo./Photodisc. 117 (bl) Werner Forman/Art Resource; (br)Richard Cummins/ SuperStock. 118 Bob Daemmrich/The Image Works. 119 (tl) David Young-Wolff/Photo Edit; (tr) David Stoecklein/Corbis. 120 Garry Black/Masterfile. 121 (l) Maxine Cass; (r) Ariel Skelley/Masterfile. 126–127 Palmer Kane Studios. 128–129 (bc) Roy Morsch/Corbis. 128 (l) Steve Essig/Index Stock Imagery/PictureQuest. 128 (r) Lawrence Migdale/Stone/ Getty Images. 129 (tr) Diaphor Agency/Index Stock Imagery. 132 (b) C Squared Studios/Photodisc/Getty Images; (c) Photodisc/Punch-Stock; (t) Wonderfile/Masterfile. 140 (bl) Charles Gupton/Corbis; (br) Michael Newman/Photo Edit. 141 (cl) Kevin Dodge/Masterfile; (tr) Corbis. 142 Craig Kojima. 143 (t) Natalie Fobes/Getty Images. 146 (b) Ariel Skelley/Masterfile; (cr) Hal Lott/Corbis; (lc) Kerrick James Photography/Stone/Getty Images. 152 (b) Creasource/ Series/PictureQuest. 153 (bl) Felicia Martinez/Photo Edit. 153 (br) Fabrik Studios/Index Stock Imagery; (c) Comstock/ PunchStock; (cr) HIRB/Index Stock Imagery; (lc) Photodisc/ Getty Images; (tl) Corbis. (tr) Spencer Grant/Photo Edit. 154 Wonderfile. 156 Sheila Rock/EMI Classics/ICM Artists Ltd. 157 Courtesy of Maria and Fernando Bujones. 158 Photodisc Collection/Getty Images. 160 (l) Steve Vidler/SuperStock; (r) Richard T. Nowitz/Corbis. 161 (l) Dynamic Graphics/Creatas. 172–173 Palmer Kane Studios. 174 (l) Corbis; (r) Rick Egan. 175 (l) Premium Stock/Corbis; (r) Rob & Sas/Corbis. 176 (cr) Photo Link/Photodisc/Picturequest; (r) Chris Windsor/Photodisc Getty Images. 177 (b) Norbert Schaefer/Corbis; (c) The Image Bank/Getty Images; (t) The Image Bank/Getty Images. 178 (c) Nancy Brown/ Getty Images; (t) Scott Vincent. 179 (lc) Bruce Coleman; (tl) Digital Vision/Getty Images. 186 David Muench/Corbis. 187 Kevin Flemming/Corbis. 188 (leaves) Siede Preis/Photodisc/ Getty Images. 189 Siede Preis/Photodisc/Getty Images. 188–189 (bkgd) Adam Jones/Taxi/Getty Images. 190 Bettmann/Corbis. 194 Dennis MacDonald/Photo Edit. 195 Jose Luis Pelaez, Inc./Corbis. 204 (bl) Dennis Thompson/Unicorn Stock Photo; (cl) Blackwell History of Education; (computer) Ryan McVay/Photodisc/Getty Images; (notebook) ©HMCo./Joe Atlas/Brand X; (pens) Corbis. 205 Jose Luis Pelaez, Inc./Corbis. 206–207 Blackwell History of Education. 208 Bridgeman Art Library. 209 Bettmann/Corbis. 210 (l) Corbis; (r) Charles Benes/Index Stock Imagery/PictureQuest. 211 (l) Tom Brakefield/Corbis; (r) Stone/Getty Images. 212–213 Roy Ooms/Masterfile. 214 (br) SW Productions/ Brand X Pictures/Getty Images. 215 (c) Bob Daemmrich/ Photo Edit; (l) Richard Hutchings/Photo Edit. 216 Jeff Greenberg/Photo Edit. 217 Jaqui Hurst/Corbis. 218 (b) ©HMCo./ Comstock; (tl) Underwood & Underwood/Corbis; (tr) Davies + Starr/Imagebank/Getty Images. 219 (c) Tom Wagner/ Corbis; (tl) Nasa; (tr) Guy Grenier/Masterfile. 224 Paul Barton/Corbis. 226–227 Jerry Tobias/Corbis. 228 (t) Stephen Chernin/Stringer/Getty Images; (r) Corbis. 229 (l) Andy Sacks/Stone/Getty Images; (r) Corbis. 231 David Young-Wolff/Photo Edit. 233 (c) Photodisc/Getty Images. 237 (b) Miles Ertman/Masterfile; (c) Gibson Stock Photography; (t) Jeff Greenberg's Collection/Index Stock Imagery. 238 (br) AP World Wide Photo; (tl) Courtesy of the City of Detroit Mayor's Office. 239 Reuters New Media Inc. 242 Tony Freeman/Photo Edit. 243 Bettman/Corbis. 245 The Greater Boston Food Bank. 250 Hulton Archive/Getty Images. 251 (b) Bettman/Corbis; (t) Corbis 252 (b) Arthur Schatz/Time Life Pictures/Getty Images; (t) Stock Montage/Superstock. 253 Hulton–Deutsch Collection/Corbis. 254–255 Photri/Microstock. 255 (tr) Courtesy of the Seeing Eye School, Morristown, NJ. 258 Burke/Triolo/Brand X Pictures/Getty Images. 259 James Lafayette/Index Stock Imagery. 260 (l) Henryk T. Kaiser/Index Stock Imagery. 261 (tr) Jeff Vanuga/Corbis. 262 Hillary Wilkes/International Stock. 263 (l) John Lawrence/Stone/Getty Images; (l) Peter Gridley/Taxi/Getty Images; (r) Corbis. 266 (l) Richard Hutchings/Photo Edit; (r) David Young–Wolff/Photo Edit. 268 Courtesy of Historical Society of Pennsylvania Collection /Bridgeman Art Library. 271 Dagli Orti/Museo de la Torre del Oro Seville/The Art Archive. 272 Rick Bowmer/AP Photo. 273 Kevin Fleming/Corbis. 274 CNP/Archive Photos/Hulton Archive/ Getty Images. 275 (r) Bettmann/Corbis; (l) Christie's Images/Corbis; (frame) ©HMCo/Image Farm. 276 Bettmann/ Corbis. 277 Ariel Skelley/Corbis. 278 IPS/Photonica. 332 (c) Davies and Starr/The Image Bank/Getty Images; (tl) Gibson Stock Photography. 333 Ronnie Kaufman/Corbis. 334 (cr) © The Nobel Foundation; (tr) Hulton–Deutsch Collection/ Corbis. 335 (cr) Corbis Corbis; (cr, frame) ©HMCo./ Photodisc/Getty images; (tl) The Granger Collection. 336 (tl) Philip James Corwin/Corbis. 337 Stone/Getty Images. 338 Maroon/Folio Inc.

Assignment Photography Credits

41 ©HMCo./Ken Karp. 74 ©HMCo./Ken Karp. 85 ©HMCo./Ken Karp. 110 ©HMCo./Ken Karp. 115 ©HMCo./Ken Karp. 130 ©HMCo./Ken Karp. 133–137 ©HMCo./Ken Karp. 145 ©HMCo./Ken Karp. 148–149 ©HMCo./Ken Karp. 161 r ©HMCo./Ken Karp. 180–181 ©HMCo./Ken Karp. 233 (t) ©HMCo./Carol Kaplan Photography. 233 (b) ©HMCo./Carol Kaplan Photograpy. 244 ©HMCo./Jade Albert. 246 ©HMCo./Ken Karp. 265 ©HMCo./Angela Coppola. 335 (br) ©HMCo./Jade Albert.

Illustration Credits

All cartographic maps done by Ortelious Design. 26–27 (borders) Sally Vitsky. 34–35 Chris Lensch. 37–38 (borders) Mircea Catusanu. 39 Jeffrey Mangiat. 40–41 Christiane Beauregard. 61 Leah Palmer Preiss. 66 Hector Borlasca. 68 Chris Lensch. 78–79 Michael Maydak. 82–83 Tracy Sabin. 85 Tracy Sabin. 86 Ron Berg. 95 Mircea Catusanu. 96 Sally Vitsky. 98–99 Mircea Catusanu. 100 Alex Burnet. 104–105 Suzanne Muse. 120–121 (flags) Patrick Gnan. 122 Hector Borlasca. 131 Cheryl Mendenhall. 133 Nathan Jarvis. 134–135 Carly Castillon. 138–139 Sally Vitsky. 151 Mark & Rosemary Jarman. 153–155 Christiane Beauregard. 156–157 Steve Costanza. 162–165 Laurence Cleyet–Merle. 172 Promotion Studios. 180–181 Mark & Rosemary Jarman. 182–183 Chris Lensch. 184–185 Robert Van Nutt. 191 Robert Van Nutt. 200–201 Cheryl Mendenhall. 202–203 Phil Wilson. 206 Patrick Gnan. 220–221 Frank Riccio. 222 Stephen Lewis. 224 Robert Van Nutt. 268 Chris Lensch.

Acknowledgments

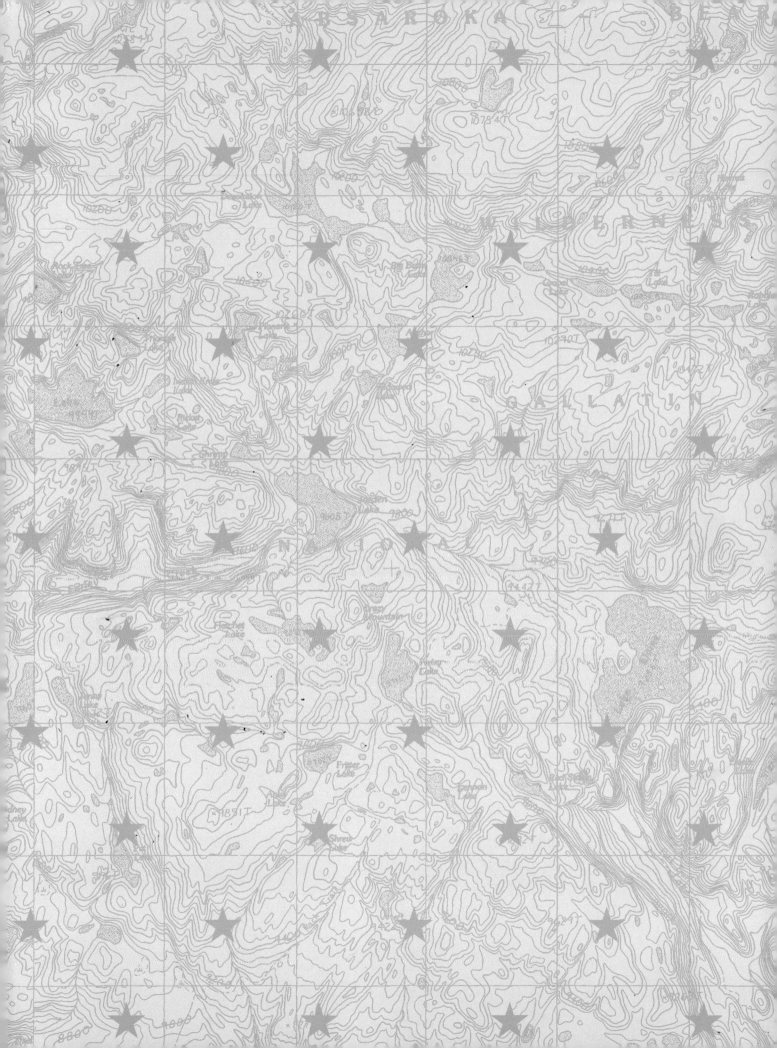